WITHDRAWN

Thinking Straight and Talking Sense

Thinking Straight and Talking Sense

AN EMOTIONAL EDUCATION PROGRAM

Mark Gerald and William Eyman

INSTITUTE FOR RATIONAL LIVING
New York

First printing, 1981
Copyright © 1981 by Institute for Rational Living, Inc.

All rights reserved. No part of this book may be reproduced in any form or by any means, except for the inclusion of brief quotations in a review, without permission in writing from the publisher.

Published by Institute for Rational Living, Inc.
45 East 65th Street, New York, New York 10021

PRINTED IN THE UNITED STATES OF AMERICA

Library of Congress Catalog Card No. 78-71008
ISBN 0-917476-14-X
EDITED BY EILEEN BRAND

Text Design by Antler & Baldwin, Inc.

Contents

The Fable of Ralph Ram:
   An Introduction to
   Rational-Emotive Education   1
Using This Book   5
Checking Up   8

PART I: Basic Language and Concept Skills

Getting Ready   10
Pretest   12

1 Sifting Facts from Opinions   14
2 Conditions Make a Difference   21
3 Relating Roger   25
4 Describing Instead of Labeling   28
5 More About Labels   32
6 The One and Only You in Many Groups   36
7 Context Makes a Difference   38
8 Smoke in the Sky — Bread on the Table?   44
9 What About Feelings?   48
10 How Events and Thoughts Affect Feelings   51
11 Who Causes Your Feelings?   57
12 Getting Rational   61
13 Your Credo   68

PART II: Problem-Solving Skills

A Word About Problems and How to Solve Them   76
Pretest   78

14	Looking at Your Skills	82
15	Learning from a Master Nasty List	85
16	Test-Making Can Be Fun	91
17	Tournaments and Contests	101
18	Advertising Your Talents	107
19	Guessing	112
20	Finding Tools for Change	116
21	The Case Against Trying	120
22	Feeling Happy — Feeling Sad	126
23	Communicating Clearly	131
24	Taking Risks	140
25	Errors, Goofs, and Blunders	145
26	Dealing with Shame	148
27	Challenging Stereotypes	152
28	Winning and Losing	156
29	Making a Game of Insults	160
30	Facing Complications	164
31	Using Your Imagination	167
32	Looking Ahead	173

How This Course Evolved   178
Reading List   179
Acknowledgments   182
About the Authors   184

Thinking Straight and Talking Sense

The Fable of Ralph Ram

An Introduction to Rational-Emotive Education

In this fable, eleven characters hear Ralph Ram say the same thing at the same time, but they respond with eleven different ways of thinking and feeling.

Ralph Ram was shouting at the flock. "It's time for us to take a stand on our two hind hoofs. Why should we follow the flock all the time? We're tired of it. We need something more than the boring life of a barnyard sheep — more than following the same old paths around the farm with the shepherd watching everything we do and the dog nipping at our heels all the time. We want freedom to roam, to explore, to experience. We want to know life the way a snake, a fox, a moth, a bat, a gnu knows it!"

"Baa-a-a-a-n that ram!" one sheep yelled.

"Baa-a-a-a-ck him up!" shouted others.

"Are you sheep or are you lemmings?" Ralph asked.

A hush fell over the flock. All the sheep — rams and ewes alike — considered what Ralph had said. Some spoke out loud about their **thoughts** and **feelings.** Others talked silently to themselves, like Great-Grandma Sheep. She said to herself, "That young whippersnapper is something else. He thinks he's the only one ever came up with an original idea. I had those same radical thoughts thirty years ago. But I found out mighty soon they wouldn't work. They couldn't work then and they won't work now." She felt **superior.**

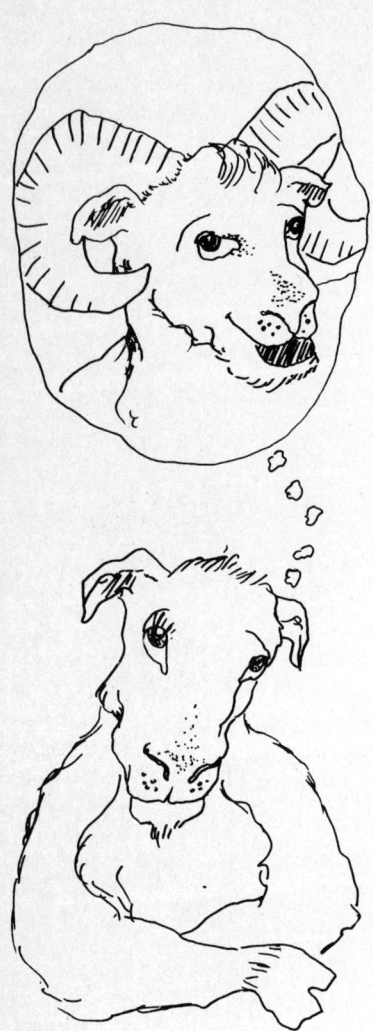

Brother Sheep shouted, "Wow, hey sheep, what's happening? We finally got a brother who got enough horns to say what's got to be said. Animals of the farm unite! Brave Ralph Ram, you are my main ram!" He felt **excited.**

May Ewe thought, "That Ralph's just the most handsome and intelligent young sheep I've ever met. Every word he says makes my wool curl up real tight." She decided she was feeling **love.**

Shirley Sheep, Ralph's mother, mused, "I don't quite understand what my Ralphie is saying or what it all means for us sheep, but he's my son and I'm for him and *everyone's* listening to him." She felt **proud.**

Waldo Ram told himself, "Ralph's a nice guy but he sure is naïve. The people that run this place will make lamb chops out of him. Forget it! I'm on good terms with the shepherd and I plan to keep things that way." He felt **aloof.**

Cherie Sheep had been deep in thought. Now she said out loud, "That Ralph, he's so good. He's always thinking of others. He's always willing to take a stand even if people make fun of him — *even if there's danger!* But why is it necessary to take such risks? Oh, why can't the world be different?" She felt **sad.**

Other farm creatures heard Ralph's words and had their own reactions.

Gene the Shepherd thought to himself, "This sheep is a wise guy. Why did I ever get into this kind of work? I should've listened to my father and been a windmill repairman." He felt **miserable.**

Gilbert Fox, lying quietly in his lair, thought, "What a fool that sheep is! This is finer than my fondest dreams . . . silly, defenseless sheep roaming alone through the countryside waiting — no, *begging* — to be picked off one by one." He felt **thrilled.**

Connie Collie sighed, "Oh, boy! Just when I've got all the strays in line, this troublemaker comes along to ruin the whole plan. If I can't keep these sheep under my paw, I'll lose my job." She felt **disgusted.**

Syd Citizen proclaimed, "What? Sheep on the loose? In our community? Why, before long, sheep will be shedding everywhere. They'll stop traffic. They'll tramp on the flowers. We won't be able to control anything. The place will never be the same!" He felt **afraid.**

Golda Goat jumped for joy as she said, "It's about time! I left the herd years ago and I never could understand how those sheep could stay in line. Maybe now I can teach them a thing or two about independence." She felt **smug.**

Well, there it is. You've read the fable. Do you see Ralph as
a whippersnapper?
brave?
intelligent?
handsome?
naïve?
good?
a wise guy?
a fool?
a troublemaker?
something else?

All of those words were used in the story to tell what Ralph "is." But they are just opinions. They may be biased and some (like *intelligent* and *a fool*) are outright contradictions. The only thing we know for sure about Ralph from this fable is that he's a ram who tells the sheep in his flock to take a stand for independence. What Ralph *does* can be observed by everyone. What Ralph "is" remains a matter of opinion.

What caused Brother Sheep's excitement, Waldo Ram's aloofness, and Connie Collie's disgust?

Each of them very likely would say, "*Ralph Ram and what he said.*"

But how could that be true, when Ralph Ram spoke and acted the same way for everyone to hear and see? Something else was happening because, when each character saw Ralph and heard what he said, each had a very different reaction. Each felt a different emotion, ranging from love and pride to fear and misery.

WHY?

Because all of the animals and people told

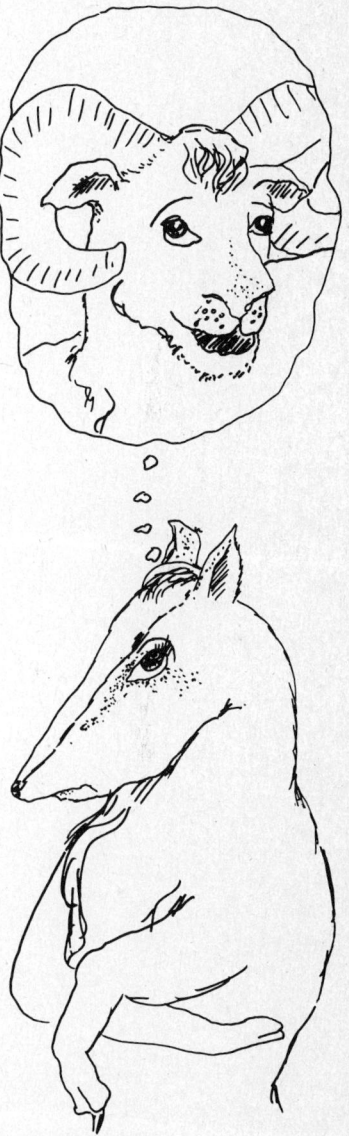

themselves something different, and this something that they told themselves — a thought or belief — caused the various feelings to occur. Suppose May Ewe told herself, "This sheep is a wise guy." Or "What a fool that sheep is!" And then suppose she said, "He'll get us all into trouble and that will be just terrible and I can't stand it!" Instead of feeling in love with Ralph Ram, she might feel terror — *even though everything Ralph Ram said and did remained the same.* The *only different thing* would have been what May Ewe told herself.

What you tell yourself affects your feelings. You can *make* yourself happy. You can *make* yourself angry or sad. You don't believe it? We'll show you more about how it's done later in this book.

We call this an emotional education program. Briefly, to educate your emotions (your feelings), here's what it takes. Learn how to get correct information. Find out what you are telling yourself about the information you get. Correct what you are telling yourself if it doesn't make sense. This may sound easy, but training yourself this way generally takes lots of practice and hard work on the lessons in this book.

We think you'll find it's worth it. You can spare yourself many kinds of trouble and get along better when you are thinking straight and talking sense to yourself as well as other people. You can get more of what you want for yourself when you are thinking straight and talking sense. And couldn't the whole world be better off if more people were thinking straight and talking sense to themselves and everybody they knew?

The fable of Ralph Ram has begun to tell you what this book is about. The fable's meaning will get clearer as you work through the exercises. Now let's see how to use this book and who can use it.

Using This Book

NOTES FOR TEACHERS

People above the fifth grade may use this book — either alone or in classes or groups. We have written simply, so people of most ages can understand it.

This introductory section will help you and your students develop a sense of what this book is about. Go over the relevant questions and answers with your class now. It may have only limited meaning at first while all the information is new, so go back over this material from time to time during the course. This section contains basic concepts that will become more and more meaningful to your students as they work through the course.

Many teachers report that the concepts included here have helped them in their personal and professional life. Use them, enjoy them, adapt them to your classes' needs, make them yours!

QUESTIONS AND ANSWERS FOR STUDENTS AND TEACHERS

Is there a name for what this book teaches?

Yes. It's called Rational-Emotive Education — REE for short. It is based on a system developed by Dr. Albert Ellis called Rational-Emotive Therapy (RET). It is used widely by counselors and psychotherapists and psychologists to help people learn how to solve their problems and live more effective lives.

What does *rational* mean?

Some of the meanings the dictionary gives are: reasonable, sensible, intelligent, wise, judicious, sane, lucid, having sound judgment, having good sense.

Some of the assignments in this book call for essays or lengthy answers, and STUDENTS WILL NEED A SUPPLEMENTARY NOTEBOOK.

What are the ideas of Rational-Emotive Therapy that Rational-Emotive Education stresses?
- Human beings can think rationally or irrationally.
- Generally when people think rationally, they are more effective, happy, and competent. They can work better and they can play better.
- Emotional disturbance results from irrational thinking much of the time.
- Many common irrational beliefs include thoughts like this: "I can't do this for myself. Someone has to do it for me." And "I should be given everything I want just because I am so important and great." And "Things have to be exactly the way I want them, and people ought to behave exactly as I think they should, and I have to behave perfectly too." And "It's awful if things don't go right for me."

What if I never have thoughts like that?

Maybe you never do, but don't be too sure. It takes many people a long time to see that they are really telling themselves statements like that when they get upset or depressed or angry.

How do you get people to think rationally?

Through a series of activities and lessons to encourage rational thinking. These have been worked out and used and tested in classrooms with teachers and students for several years. (We tell more fully how this course developed in a section at the end of the book.) One reason these activities and lessons succeed is that our course is built on these ideas:
- You can change the ways you think and feel and behave through hard work and persistence, even though the world around you and some things about being human sometimes make it seem easy to think irrationally.
- We all experience and learn. We can keep on learning more and more from what happens to us because we have so much of that ability. Setting up lessons based on what you experience is surely as important as other studies.
- The *way* we talk and act often helps people know what we mean just as much as what we say does.
- We can figure out our long-range goals and how to work toward them. At the same time we'd better

Thinking Straight and Talking Sense

remember that short steps are as important as long steps.
- To take a first step toward changing in good ways, it often helps to take risks that make sense — *rational* risks.
- Knowing what goes on in your mind and body and how people deal with each other and affect each other can help you avoid poor mental health.
- Healthy growth of your mind and emotions comes easier when the people around you care and help you in your growth. That's why groups and classes work so well. (But many people can gain a lot by working on this course on their own. However you study it, remember it takes as much hard work and practice as it does to learn any other complex skill.)

Do you have a teacher's manual for this course?

No. Each lesson has *Notes for Teachers.* We wrote them with teachers in mind, but the notes can help learners too.

Should this course be taught as a special course or should it be used in connection with other classes?

Either way. For teachers with little or no background in Rational-Emotive Education, it usually works best to present the basics that you find in Part I in a separate and special class. Once you are comfortable with the material in Part I, you can make it part of other subject areas. As you use it in science, reading, anthropology, ethnic studies, creative writing, or social studies, you can begin to develop new lessons based on the interests, learning levels, and experiences of the class. Use this approach, too, with classroom problems. When fights, jealousies, withdrawals, and other stresses come up, deal with them by using the concepts and methods shown in this book. Applying the information in this course to many areas and activities provides practical means of reinforcing the lessons learned here.

Are there books I can read that will give me a good background for this course?

Yes. You will find a reading list in the back of this book. Two good basic works are *A New Guide to Rational Living* by Albert Ellis and Robert A. Harper, and *Rational Counseling Primer* by Howard Young. The list includes books for young children as well as adults.

Checking Up

As you work through this course, you may find it hard to see the relationship of a single activity to the major concepts of this book. Yet as you go along you will find that each exercise adds to your understanding. To help tie all the lessons to the basics of this course, we have developed a series of questions that you can use to check yourself with each lesson. We suggest that you make these a habit.

1. *What am I doing?*
   Describe to another person what you think you're doing and check it out.
2. *What do I want to get out of this?*
   State your goal — as obvious, simple, or complex as you want to make it.
3. *How do I feel about what I'm doing?*
   Usually one or two emotional terms will answer this.
4. *What do I think about what I'm doing?*
   What sentence or sentences are you saying in your head?
5. *Am I getting what I want?*
   Go back to your answer to Question 2, and answer Yes or No to this question.
6. *If not, would it help if I changed my thinking?*
   We think so. Try it and see.
7. *How can I do that?*
   It probably won't happen all at once. Going over each exercise several times, talking about the exercises with other people, practicing the lessons you have learned — all are good ways to begin to change your thinking.

PART 1
Basic Language and Concept Skills

Getting Ready

RECENTLY a friend of ours who is healthy, strong, and good in sports played his first game of basketball. Everyone thought he'd make a great team member. After all, he had what it takes, they told each other. But guess what happened! He tripped, fumbled, fell, shot too hard, passed to the other team, and generally did a lot to help his team lose. Afterward, the team was sorry they had chosen him. So was he. Why? Because even though he had the *potential* (he could *learn* to be a good basketball player), he didn't have the *skill*. How *could* he have played well in that first game? *No way*.

People have the same problem when they start this course. When we first began presenting course activities to our students, we sat them down in a circle and asked them to talk about what bothered them. We expected them to have so much to talk about that there wouldn't be time to cover it all. Instead . . . silence. Then . . . a bit of strained talking. When we questioned each student alone afterward, we heard words like *boring* . . . *uncomfortable* . . . *scary* . . . *confusing*. When we dug deeper, we found what our friend's teammates found — a lack of skills. We learned that they didn't understand some of the words we were saying and some of the concepts or ideas we were presenting. Not only did they not understand what we were saying, they didn't have the words to speak of complex things in their lives. Many of them didn't know

- the difference between a *fact* and an *opinion*
- what an *assumption* is

Notes for TEACHERS

This section is mainly for you, but we think you will find that a discussion of it with your group will serve to enhance their understanding of the function of this course.

- what an *alternative* or *option* is
- the difference between *conditional* and *absolute*
- the part *context* plays in what we understand about something
- what a *behavior* is
- the concepts of *cause* and *effect*
- the meanings of *event, belief, thought, feeling*

So we backed up and decided to begin by developing the skills that would help people deal more clearly with the problems in their lives. The activities that follow in Part I provide the language and other tools to develop skills in solving problems and in clarifying concepts and ideas. What impressed us most was finding that many students, once they had mastered the words, could label concepts that they had understood all the time but couldn't name.

If learning what certain words mean is so important, why don't we just jot down a few dictionary definitions and save some time?

A good question. Our answer is that there is a good deal more to understanding concepts than simply having the dictionary meaning. Many people can tell you what a fact is and what an opinion is — the way the dictionary does. But in their ordinary thinking and talking they don't sort out the differences between facts and opinions very clearly. It takes training to do that, and the exercises we've included in Part I can deepen your understanding of certain concepts and develop your thinking and communicating skills.

Children as well as adults have lives rich in events, and specific conceptual skills can bridge the gap between raw experience, understanding, and growth. Let's begin to develop those skills by finding out what we know and what we don't know about some of the things to learn in this course. To do that, we use a Pretest. It's a good idea to give the test when you start Part I, and then go back and review it after you've finished Part I. That way you can see how much your group has learned.

Pretest

Notes for TEACHERS

Teachers with whom we have worked have suggested a pretest of the concepts introduced in this unit in order to assess student familiarity. Below are some of the pretest questions we've asked. (They are followed by

Pretest for Students

1. Allan accurately reported, "Yesterday, my friend Gary wasn't in school." Which of the following statements would be facts with regard to that first sentence?

    a. ___ Gary wasn't in school yesterday.

    b. ___ Gary was sick yesterday.

    c. ___ Allen wasn't in school yesterday.

2. Change the following absolute statement to a less absolute, more conditional statement: "Learning is fun."

    _____

3. Can you tell what the word "epfurg" means in the following sentence? "I lifted my epfurg and walked away." Yes ___ No ___ Why or why not? _____

    _____

4. Place an X next to each statement which says what someone *does*:

    a. ___ Louis is a good student.

    b. ___ Louis studies four hours almost every day.

    c. ___ Sharon has a C.B. radio.

    d. ___ Sharon talks on her C.B. radio every night at 10:00.

5. Read the following statement:
"Aunt Rose kissed Jeffrey and he got a cold."
Now place an X on each statement that is clearly true.

    a. ___ Jeffrey got a cold from Aunt Rose.

    b. ___ Aunt Rose had a cold.

    c. ___ Jeffrey is in generally poor health.

    d. ___ Kisses cause colds.

answers to these pretest questions.) We urge you to use this list and expand upon it. These same questions along with others you may think of can be used at the end of each unit to assess the student's mastery of the material presented.

6. Read the following statement:
   "Our thoughts determine our feelings about things that happen to us."
   Do you agree or disagree with this statement?

   __ Agree   __ Disagree

7. In the following sequences, label the events (A), the thoughts (B), and the feelings (C).
   Sequence 1 ( ) I got $10 for my birthday.
              ( ) I wonder what they want from me.
              ( ) Anger.
   Sequence 2 ( ) I got $10 for my birthday.
              ( ) Wow! I know they can't afford this, but what a nice thing to do!
              ( ) Gratitude.

8. In question 7, why did the two persons feel differently about the same event? _____
   _____
   _____

Key to Answers to Questions in Pretest

1. a.
2. "Learning is fun for some people."
   or
   "I often think learning is fun."
   or
   "A lot of people consider learning fun."
3. No, because the CONTEXT gives very few clues.
4. b., d.
5. None of them.
6. When you are asked whether you agree or disagree with an answer, any truthful answer is correct. As to the statement in Question 6, people who understand REE theory would agree that it is true.
7. Sequence 1 (A)   Sequence 2 (A)
              (B)   (B)
              (C)   (C)
8. Because they had different thoughts.

1 Sifting Facts from Opinions

NOTES FOR TEACHERS

Since few adults carefully sort out facts from opinions at all times, this lesson offers a challenge to teachers and adult groups as well as teen-agers and elementary pupils.

Use the first few paragraphs of this lesson to introduce the concepts of fact and opinion. You may find our brief discussion enough to allow the group to go on to the exercises, or you may want to expand on it. The definition of *fact* raises all sorts of questions. As questions come up, it is a good idea to write them down. Discuss them briefly as they come up, but let the group know that you will go back to them after everyone has done the question-and-answer section.

Notes for Students

What's a *fact*? Thinkers have puzzled over this question for centuries. Here's the definition we have gotten the most agreement for:

A *fact* is a physical phenomenon — or an act by a living thing — that people can observe and verify. It is NOT:

an idea
a theory
a hypothesis
an opinion
a thought
a feeling
a sense
some vibes
a prediction

Observe and *verify* — what do they mean? When people *observe* something, they can see it, hear it, touch it, smell it, or taste it. Sometimes they can do all of those things, sometimes only one or two of them. It depends on the fact they are observing. Generally, when something is a fact, *other* people can see, hear, touch, smell, or taste the same thing you can. When they agree on a fact because of what their senses tell them, they *verify* it. You also can *verify* something for yourself by checking to see if your senses give you the same information that they did before.

Sometimes we're *sure* we've got the facts until someone points out that we've just made an assumption. (Making an *assumption* means you are guessing or supposing or taking for granted.) What we thought was a fact (we could've *sworn* it) was really an opinion. (There's nothing wrong with having an opinion, of course, as long as you tell yourself and other people that it's *just* your opinion and could stand some checking out.) The following story and questions about it will give you some good practice in sorting out facts from opinions and assumptions.

• •

Read this story carefully.

ON Tuesday, October 9th, I got a call from Lorraine Callahan inviting me to a party at her house the following Saturday. I didn't really want to go, so I told her I was busy. On Thursday I ran into Willie Mason at the Country Corner Shopping Center and he asked me if I wanted to go to a party with him. I said I did but I didn't get any details because he had to leave. When he called me Saturday morning, he told me that the party was at the house of someone he had just met and he couldn't remember her name. When we got there, it turned out to be Lorraine Callahan's.

Now, read each of the following statements. If you are *absolutely* sure a statement is true, circle the T. If you are absolutely sure it is false, circle the F. Otherwise circle the question mark (?).

1. The person speaking is female.
    ?   T   F

2. Lorraine and the person speaking are good friends.
    ?   T   F

3. Lorraine was planning a big party.
    ?   T   F

Sifting Facts from Opinions

4. The person speaking doesn't like Lorraine.
    ?   T   F
 5. Lorraine's parties are dull.
    ?   T   F
 6. Lorraine is a teen-ager.
    ?   T   F
 7. The person speaking is honest.
    ?   T   F
 8. The person speaking said (s)he didn't want to go to the party.
    ?   T   F
 9. The person speaking had planned to do something on Saturday.
    ?   T   F
10. Willie Mason and the person speaking often go shopping.
    ?   T   F
11. Willie Mason is a male.
    ?   T   F
12. There are often parties at Lorraine Callahan's.
    ?   T   F
13. The person speaking likes parties.
    ?   T   F
14. Willie was shopping when the person speaking met Willie.
    ?   T   F
15. Willie invited him or her to a party.
    ?   T   F
16. Willie is always in a hurry.
    ?   T   F
17. The person speaking accepted the invitation.
    ?   T   F
18. Willie and Lorraine had just met.
    ?   T   F
19. The person speaking and Willie went to the party together.
    ?   T   F
20. The person speaking was surprised and embarrassed to see Lorraine.
    ?   T   F

Here are the correct answers.

1. ?	6. ?	11. T	16. ?
2. ?	7. ?	12. ?	17. T
3. ?	8. T	13. ?	18. ?
4. ?	9. ?	14. ?	19. ?
5. ?	10. ?	15. T	20. ?

Some of you are probably confused now. You were SURE that number 7 was *false.* After all, the person speaking did not tell Lorraine the truth — but all we can say for sure is that the person speaking *did not communicate honestly* in *this* situation.

A little clearer? Now, look back over the story and see if you can decide why the correct answers were as we gave them. Discuss them with your classmates. Then, when you've come to the end of your rope, read the following explanations:

1. ? Maybe. Maybe not. We can't be *sure.*
2. ? Same as number 1.
3. ? Same as number 1.
4. ? Same as number 1. Maybe (s)he likes Lorraine, but just doesn't want to go to *this* party.
5. ? Same as number 1.
6. ? Same as number 1.
7. ? Same as number 1.
8. True. The person speaking *said* it.
9. ? The speaker said so, but whether (s)he *did* or not is another story.
10. ? Same as number 1.
11. True. The story says "he had to leave."
12. ? Same as number 1.
13. ? Same as number 1.
14. ? Same as number 1. Maybe he was *working* there.
15. True.
16. ? Same as number 1.
17. True.
18. ? We know that Willie said it, but do we know that it is true?
19. ? Same as number 1. They both *got* there, but did they *go* together?
20. ? Same as number 1.

Read each of the following statements and decide which is a *fact* and which is *not a fact.*
1. Some New Yorkers live in apartments.
Yes. That is a fact.
2. New Yorkers live in apartments.
All New Yorkers? No! So the second statement *can't* be a fact.

Now read these sentences and write Yes after a statement that is a *fact* and No after a statement that is *not a fact.*

1. Dogs are animals. _____

Sifting Facts from Opinions

2. Dogs run fast. _____
3. The Atlantic Ocean is east of the United States of America. _____
4. The Atlantic Ocean is the most beautiful sea in the world. _____
5. Some folks consider the Atlantic the world's most beautiful ocean. _____
6. Hamburgers are a popular food in many American restaurants. _____
7. Hamburgers have meat in them. _____
8. Hamburgers taste great. _____
9. Spiders are ugly. _____
10. Spiders are smaller than dinosaurs. _____
11. Spiders bite kids. _____
12. This is a really hard lesson. _____

Here are the correct answers:
1. Yes.
2. No. Not *all* dogs *all* the time.
3. Yes.
4. No. Not *all* people agree.
5. Yes. Some *do.*
6. Yes.
7. Yes.
8. No. Not to everyone.
9. No. *Some* people consider them beautiful.
10. Yes.
11. No. Not *all* spiders, not *all* kids, not *always*. That sentence needs a qualifying word like *sometimes* to make it a fact.
12. No. For *some* it's probably easy.

Notes for Students

What's an *opinion*?

An *opinion* is a belief that someone has about someone or something without having enough information to show it is a fact.

Here are two sentences. One's an opinion; one's a fact.

Gary's a fool! An OPINION — not observable, not verifiable.

Michele said, "Gary's a fool." A FACT — she *did* say it, several people heard her and they all reported the same statement. Now this doesn't *mean* Gary's a fool. But it does mean that Michele said it.

ACTIVITY ACTIVITY ACTIVITY

CHECK the statements below that you're sure are facts — that is, that you can observe and verify and prove them.

1. New York is a city. ___
2. New York is the greatest city in the world. ___
3. Some people say New York is the greatest city in the world. ___
4. New York is not a great city. ___
5. New York will always be a city. ___

"New York is a city" and "Some people say New York is the greatest city in the world" are facts. Did you check them?

All the other statements are opinions.

And, as a matter of fact, "New York is a city" is not just that one single fact because New York is also a state. And a county.

NOTES FOR TEACHERS

A teacher we know makes a class game — "Fact or Not?" — of challenging statements every day. He asks someone for a statement. Then he asks, "Fact or not?" and calls for qualifiers to make absolute statements more *conditionally* true. The game goes like this:

    Someone says, "It's three o'clock."
    The teacher asks, "Fact or not?"
    Someone responds, "Fact."
    The teacher asks, "All over the world?"
    Someone answers, "In our time zone."

The teacher and class repeat this process until they have considered ten statements.

LIBRARY

Sifting Facts from Opinions

Notes for Students

Begin considering the statements you make. Ask yourself, "Fact or not?" Is a statement an *absolute* truth? Is it true for all times and all places and all people? If it isn't, what conditions or qualifying words can you add that will make it a true statement — a fact?

Examine your class lessons in the same way. History is especially hard to verify. Did Christopher Columbus discover America? Some history books say he did. Other histories name someone else. In cases like this, where you cannot *personally* verify something, you can give the *source* of your information. You can say, "according to my history book," and then go on to repeat the information provided in your book. That way you will show that you have learned the information there but you will avoid stating it as an unconditional fact.

2 Conditions Make a Difference

NOTES FOR TEACHERS

This unit expands on the concept of the fact by dealing with absolute and conditional concepts. Give ample time to this unit, add your own insights and examples to the ideas included here, and refer often to the information in Unit 1 as the foundation for the material here.

Notes for Students

Sometimes a fact is a fact no matter what — but often something we think is a fact changes with different conditions. The closer we look, the more clearly we see that an *absolute* (what appears true for everyone in all conditions) is often not so absolute. This lesson helps teach the difference between what's *conditional* (depends on the conditions) and what's absolute. This lesson also provides a basis for understanding the terms *rational* and *irrational*. We said a little bit about those terms at the beginning of this book. Later on, we'll really work on them.

HERE'S an absolute statement: SCHOOL IS FUN!

School is fun! means *everything* about school is *always* fun. Do you agree?

Ask ten students the question, *"Do you think school is fun?"* Write their answers in your notebook.

Did anyone give you a CONDITIONAL answer, such as *sometimes* or *when I feel good* or *in Mr. Lansford's class* or *at lunch time* or *as long as I do my homework* or *if I understand the work* or *if Joe is absent* or *not usually but once in a while* or *depends* or *during breaks*?

Here's another statement to consider: TEACHERS KNOW MORE THAN KIDS.

Is that statement true? Is it false? Or would you say, "It depends."

ABSOLUTE   TRUE means — ALL teachers know more than ALL students ALL OF THE TIME.
FALSE means — NO teacher knows more than ANY student EVER.

CONDITIONAL   IT DEPENDS means — Sure, in *some* CONDITIONS, CIRCUMSTANCES, or POINTS OF VIEW, teachers *do* know more than kids, but not ALL teachers ALL of the time.

Check the statements below that you think are true.
1. Some teachers know a lot more about math than many students. ____
2. Many teachers know much more about grammar than most students. ____
3. A lot of teachers know more about vocabulary than most students. ____

Notes for Students

We'd expect most people to check all three statements because we added CONDITIONS.

Let's go back to our ABSOLUTE statement: TEACHERS KNOW MORE THAN KIDS.

That statement CAN'T be true because ALL teachers *don't* know more than ALL students ALL OF THE TIME.

As one small example, you probably know MUCH MORE about your family, your neighborhood, and your best friend than *any* of your teachers. And, of course, your teacher knows MUCH MORE about SOME things than you do.

Here are some ABSOLUTE statements we've heard and then changed to CONDITIONAL statements. The conditions are in heavy letters:
1. Nebraska's great.
   Kathy says Nebraska's great.
2. Girls are physically weak.

Some girls are physically weak. (So are **some** boys.)
3. Americans make a lot of money.
   Many Americans make a lot of money. (**Many** don't.)
4. People who live on the lake have boats.
   Most people who live on the lake have boats. (**Some** don't.)
5. Black people want the same things white people want.
   A lot of black people want the same things **many** white people want.

Here is a list of words and phrases that put *conditions* or *qualifications* on absolute statements:

WHO?	WHEN?	WHERE?	WHAT?
some	sometimes	some places	some
someone	once in a while	many places	many
many		most places	most
most	on Tuesdays	few places	few
a lot of	at noon	in Ohio	a few
a majority	when	at Sunbury	a majority of
a few	whenever	on U.S. 36	not many
several	occasionally	on earth	almost none
not many	seldom	at school	scarcely any
	usually		
	often		
	mostly		
	almost never		
	almost always		

We could go on and on, but you've probably got the point by now.

• •

REWRITE the following sentences, adding words that change the statements from *absolute* to *conditional*.

1. June's a beautiful month.

EXAMPLE: June's *often* a beautiful month. Or: *Last year* June was a beautiful month, *as I remember it.*

2. Greeks are dark. _____
3. Miami is modern. _____
4. Sugar is no good for you. _____
   _____
5. Math's easy. _____

Conditions Make a Difference

6. Young men run fast. ⎯⎯⎯⎯⎯

7. Time flies. ⎯⎯⎯⎯⎯

8. You can't teach an old dog new tricks. ⎯⎯⎯⎯⎯
⎯⎯⎯⎯⎯

9. Nice guys finish last. ⎯⎯⎯⎯⎯
⎯⎯⎯⎯⎯

10. The best things in life are free. ⎯⎯⎯⎯⎯
⎯⎯⎯⎯⎯

There are some other ways of qualifying a statement. You can add phrases like *I think* or *it seems to me* or *I believe* or *it appears* or *as far as I can tell* or *I guess* or *I see.*

Other common qualifiers are *if . . . but . . . however . . . on the other hand . . . although . . . even though . . . even if . . . maybe . . . perhaps . . . possibly . . . probably.*

Here's a suggestion that has helped several classes and individuals we know to sort out absolute and conditional statements:

Make a wall chart of all the qualifying words and phrases you can think of and hang it up so you'll see it every day. Begin to point to and use the qualifying words and phrases in the written and oral language of your school class or group. Don't make a big deal of it, but if you do it a little at a time, you'll notice a difference in your language — and in your thinking.

3 Relating Roger

NOTES FOR TEACHERS

Roger's many roles (and the activities we suggest) provide a springboard for a mind-stretching discussion of roles. How many students see their teachers as people who have lives and concerns far beyond the classroom? How many children see their parents as people whose feelings and interests extend far beyond their children? How many parents see their children as individuals — persons with an identity other than "my son" or "my daughter"?

Notes for Students

Who IS Roger?

Hello! My name is Roger.

Who is this Roger anyway?

Roger is my brother.

No, Roger is my friend.

No, Roger is my son.

No, Roger is *my* son.

No, Roger is my student.

No, Roger is my newspaper delivery boy.

No, Roger is my employee.

No, Roger is my uncle.

Stop! Nobody's wrong. I mean different things to different people. It all depends on who's talking about me.

NOW let's talk about YOU instead of Roger.
Are YOU *always* a son or daughter to the person you're talking with?
In what circumstances are you a student?
What are you in relationship to

your aunt? _____

your grandparents? _____

a person that you don't know? _____

your dog? _____

a person on your baseball team? _____

a person in your class? _____

a person who works for you? _____

the mayor of your city? _____

a person who works in the supermarket? _____

your doctor? _____

The label you chose in each situation depends on whom or what you're relating to.

In the blank space, write either BIG or SMALL to describe yourself. _____

Now, answer the following questions:

Are you BIG or SMALL compared to
Tommy Burleson, a 7'2" basketball player? _____

The person sitting closest to you? _____

Your pen or pencil? _____

Your teacher? _____

Busch Stadium in St. Louis? _____

Yourself last year? _____

Yourself in five years? _____

A 4'1" bottle of soy sauce? _____

The Empire State Building? _____

Your youngest relative? _____

Is the word (BIG or SMALL) you used to describe yourself at the start of this activity always true? _____

26 *Thinking Straight and Talking Sense*

Complete the following sentences with as many responses as you can:

I am now bigger than

1. _____
2. _____
3. _____
4. _____
5. _____

I am now smaller than

1. _____
2. _____
3. _____
4. _____
5. _____

So ... what you think is a fact about you is not ALWAYS a fact.

Assignment for Tomorrow: In your notebook, make a list of as many of your roles as you can think of. Suppose you know Spanish and English, and people sometimes ask you to tell them what a Spanish phrase means in English. When you do, you fill the role of *translator.* Think of your hobbies and games and list your roles in doing those things. Consider your household tasks and the roles you play in doing them, and add them to your list. Then go back to the section earlier in this lesson where we said, "Now let's talk about YOU instead of Roger." We raised questions there about your roles in relationship to other people. Beginning with those suggestions, add to your list your roles in relating to other people.

4 Describing Instead of Labeling

NOTES FOR TEACHERS

As preparation for this unit, review with your class the forms of the verb *to be*, such as *is, are, am, was, were, be, been, being*. Don't forget the contractions, like *I'm* for *I am*, and *he's* for *he is*, and *you're* for *you are*. This lesson can help in the study of verbs in English grammar. As we go through this book, you will see how the activities tie into various subjects — like math and English and history. Use every opportunity to work these lessons into other areas. The goal of emotional education is to give people skills for maintaining mental health, and people don't get those skills in a vacuum. These lessons take at least as much thought and repetition and looking for new ways to use them as anything else you teach. Go over them again and again. Keep showing your students how to apply them to their daily activities.

Notes for Students

In the last lesson we asked you to make a list of all your roles. Even after you made a very long list, you probably realized it wasn't complete. That's partly because people find it hard to think of all their roles and partly because your roles and other people's roles keep changing. For example, did you think to add to your list as you prepared it that one of your roles was *role list-maker*?

Still, if someone asked you to describe yourself, saying you were a *role list-maker* wouldn't give much of a picture of you, would it? Just because you play a certain role in certain circumstances doesn't mean you *are* that role. Why not find a better way to talk about yourself and other people? Take a look at how you use *is* and *are* and other forms of *to be*.

What we say a person *is* often simply expresses an

opinion or *point of view*. Let's look at the difference between *is* and *does*:

John's a whiz! Annette's nice. You're a real brain. Sue's a lousy reader. Louie's a good guy. Could anyone prove any of those statements *absolutely* true — in all respects and for all time? Not likely. But we can list specific things that might lead you to say, for example, "Annette's nice." One of our classes kept a list of such behaviors for two days, and this is what they wrote:

Annette smiled.
Annette gave Darlene her apple for lunch.
Annette said my hair looked nice.
Annette combed my hair for me.
Annette stopped when I fell in gym and asked if I was OK.
Annette said "Hi" to Mr. Lavalle, the janitor.
Annette let me copy her English notes.

After we went over the list together in class, we had this discussion:

"OK, we'll accept that. These behaviors can be PROVED, right?"

"Right!"

"How?"

"Because you could *see* her or *hear* her doing them."

"And several people would see and hear the same thing?"

"Yes."

"Can you see her or hear her 'be nice'?"

"Well . . ."

"She IS nice means she's nice *always* under *all* conditions. Can we prove that?"

"Well . . ."

"Did she do anything in the two days that anyone considered *not* nice?"

"Yes. She laughed when Alex dropped his tray in the cafeteria."

"Really?"

"And she kicked the wall when she struck out in softball."

"Well, I don't consider either of those BEHAVIORS horrible, but I wouldn't call them 'nice.'"

"Neither would I."

Have you noticed how much this activity ties into Unit 1, SIFTING FACTS FROM OPINIONS? As we sort out facts from opinions, we see that only the BEHAVIORS in this activity can rate as facts.

Describing Instead of Labeling

READ the following statements and sort them out according to BEHAVIORS (B) and NOT BEHAVIORS (N).

1. Greg played the drums for two hours last night. ____
2. Greg's a good drummer. ____
3. Alberta cooked Spanish rice for dinner. ____
4. Alberta is the greatest cook anywhere. ____
5. I ate two helpings of her Spanish rice. ____
6. Paul and Gail went roller skating last night. ____
7. Gail doesn't skate very well. ____
8. She fell three times. ____
9. Abby works till five every day. ____
10. Abby is a very good employee. ____
11. The boss said Abby's a good worker. ____
12. Lenny ran the mile in 5:20. ____
13. Lenny's our star. ____
14. Lenny told me being a star is no big thing. ____
15. Fifteen questions are a *lot* of questions. ____

The answers are:

1. B
2. N Maybe he is, maybe he isn't, but this doesn't tell us anything he DID.
3. B
4. N Maybe, maybe not, but what did she DO?
5. B
6. B
7. N Tricky. It's possible she doesn't skate at all. This statement doesn't really tell us — it just gives us an opinion.
8. B
9. B
10. N What does she DO? Whatever it is has led someone to believe she does it well, but WHAT IS IT?
11. B He *said* it. Whether it's true or not is another matter.
12. B
13. N What has he DONE to be seen as the star?

14. B   Yes, he said it.
15. N

Now let's go back to the beginning of this unit and take another look at statements like "John's a whiz." For each one write four BEHAVIORS by the person that you think might have led someone to say what (s)he did about her or him. These will be guesses, and there's no right or wrong as long as you write down BEHAVIORS . . . actions . . . what the person *did*.

John's a whiz!
_____
_____
_____
_____

Annette's nice.
_____
_____
_____
_____

You're a real brain!
_____
_____
_____
_____

Sue's a lousy reader.
_____
_____
_____
_____

Louie's a good guy.
_____
_____
_____
_____

5 More About Labels

NOTES FOR TEACHERS

We do things. Then often we judge them. Others judge them. Sometimes we judge our whole selves, or others judge us, because of *one* thing we did. This activity, like the last one, can help people see the difference between *single behaviors* and *over-all labels*. It asks the question, "Are you any *one* thing just because of what you do?"

Notes for Students

On a single day in May, twelve-year-old Terri Ann Nelson DID the following:

got out of bed.

braided her hair.

made breakfast (poached eggs and corn bread) for herself and her three brothers and sisters.

gave herself her insulin injection.

dressed her three-year-old sister.

ironed her skirt.

walked to school.

memorized the words to a popular song she was listening to on the radio.

did Chinese jump rope for two minutes and forty-two seconds before missing.

talked to her friend Janice about baby-sitting.

refused to touch a frog and a salamander in science class.

finished a third of her math assignment and half of her language arts assignment.

sat silently during a discussion on the story in her literature book.

failed a test on kitchen measurement in home economics class.

did the family laundry and sorted and folded it.

explained the correct bus route to the North Side to a woman from her neighborhood.

walked away from a strange couple on the street who asked her for directions.

lost two games of checkers to her friend Greg.

played "Ghost" with David, Greg, Michele, Cheryl, Mark, and Dawn.

cried when she heard her friend Maria had not invited her to Maria's birthday dinner.

told her mother the birth dates of four of her cousins.

finished painting a small chest of drawers for her bedroom.

watched five minutes of TV.

showered.

went to bed.

So what *is* Terri Ann?

Is she *slow*?
Is she *helpful*?
Is she *friendly*?
Is she *dynamic*?
Is she *brave*?
Is she *dumb*?
Is she *handy*?
Is she *irresponsible*?
Is she *cautious*?
Is she *weak*?
Is she *bright*?

What do you think?

Do all of those labels apply to her all of the time?

Do some of them apply some of the time?

When do they apply?

Here's what we think —

She has been called or has called herself all of those things — SOME times in SOME circumstances.

But in Rational-Emotive Education we believe —

SHE *is* not any one of them.

When she gave directions to her neighbor, she was *behaving* in a friendly and helpful way, but when she walked away from the strangers she was *behaving* in a cautious way.

Terri Ann IS *friendly* MEANS Terri Ann IS *friendly* ALL OF THE TIME — and obviously she IS NOT.

LABELS DON'T ALWAYS HELP!

Terri Ann DOES lots of things but Terri Ann ISN'T any of them.

More About Labels 33

HERE'S an exercise for you to do with yourself: First, make a list of adjectives (descriptive words) that people have used to describe you. What have such people as your parents, brothers, sisters, teachers, classmates, friends, neighbors, relatives, doctor, paper route customers, local store owners said about you? If it helps, take a few days to compile your list with care.

Here's an example list from Marcia: *kind, boring, lovely, smart, snotty, fast, confused, lazy, rough, corny, bratty, fair, rich, nasty, silly, pretty, young-looking, strong, sad, weird.*

Write your list here or in your notebook.

_____
_____
_____
_____
_____
_____
_____
_____
_____
_____

One thing most people will notice is that there are many different labels, depending on who said what and when or in what circumstances they said it.

Do *all* of the labels apply to you *all* of the time?
Do *some* of them apply *some* of the time?
When do they apply?

Well, now, let's get serious about this. Choose a day in which you are going to write down all of the things you DO, something like the list we made for Terri Ann. Be as complete as possible. Don't use *any* describing words. For example, don't say, "I did a good job in math." Say instead, "I got a B+ in math" or "My teacher *said* I did a good job in math."

All right — begin. Plan to use a couple of pages in your notebook for this project.

After you have finished your list, choose several things that you did, and do the following activity.

Think of what another person might think about you in connection with what you did. For example:

What I Did	What Other People Might Think About Me
I played three innings of softball after school.	My friend Alex might think I was a GOOD ATHLETE.
	My neighbor, Mr. Graziano, might think I'm just another CRAZY KID.
	My mother might think I'm IRRESPONSIBLE.
	My friend's mother, Mrs. Barth, might think I'm CUTE in my uniform.

List at least five activities under "What I Did." For *each* activity write how you think at least four people would label you.

After you have finished this project, review those labels you think people would have given you. Do they accurately tell you what you are? In the example above, if Alex, Mr. Graziano, your mother, and Mrs. Barth had put those labels on you, would that mean you really *were* a good athlete, a crazy kid, irresponsible, and cute?

Now, answer these questions:

1. Are you one thing because of what you do? _____
2. Does any one adjective describe all of you? _____
3. If someone says you are something, are you that thing? _____
4. How do you feel when someone labels you negatively? _____
5. How do you feel when someone labels you positively? _____ Why? What might you be thinking?

6 The One and Only You in Many Groups

NOTES FOR TEACHERS

The following activity employs a knowledge of fractions. However, the concept can be taught to students without this knowledge by presenting a series of varying sizes of circles labeled earth, country, state, county, city, and smaller areas. Use these circles as the background for a small human figure. The size of the figure will appear to change in relation to the various backgrounds. Paper, cardboard, or felt can be used as materials for this demonstration.

Notes for Students

You live in many different orbits. You are one person in more than 4,000,000,000 — FOUR BILLION! (Actually, it's closer to four and a quarter billion, but we'll stick to round billions here.)

Each characteristic you have — your height, your skin color, your nationality, your sex — you probably share with others. But when your characteristics all are put together, you are the one and only you. Take a look at yourself.

LET'S begin with numbers. Think first of yourself as one whole person.

Now compare yourself fractionally with the following groups of people. Fill in the figure below the line, as we have done in the first example.

$$\frac{\text{you}}{\text{all the people in the world}} \qquad \frac{1}{4,000,000,000}$$

$$\frac{\text{you}}{\text{all the people in your country}} \qquad \frac{1}{}$$

$$\frac{\text{you}}{\text{all the people in your state}} \qquad \frac{1}{}$$

$$\frac{\text{you}}{\text{all the people in your city, town, village}} \qquad \frac{1}{}$$

$$\frac{\text{you}}{\text{all the people in your school}} \qquad \frac{1}{}$$

$$\frac{\text{you}}{\text{all the people in your class}} \qquad \frac{1}{}$$

$$\frac{\text{you}}{\text{all the people in your family}} \qquad \frac{1}{}$$

$$\frac{\text{you}}{\text{all the children in your family}} \qquad \frac{1}{}$$

$$\frac{\text{you}}{\text{all the people of your race in your city, town, village}} \qquad \frac{1}{}$$

See, you change — mathematically — according to the category you go into.

The One and Only You in Many Groups

7 Context Makes a Difference

NOTES FOR TEACHERS

The previous unit showed the individual in the numerical context of other people in large and small and intermediate groups. This unit expands the idea of context and emphasizes its importance in understanding our perceptions. Activities such as this can provide students with experience in critical thinking and help develop a more rational view of external and internal reality.

Notes for Students

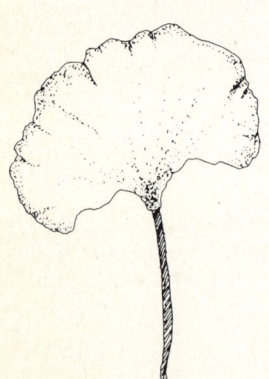

A ginkgo leaf doesn't look like any other leaf. It is shaped like a fan.

The tree came originally from eastern China, and grows elsewhere, although it is not very common in the United States. We took the outline of a ginkgo leaf and showed it to people in a park, a crafts shop, a museum, a plastics factory, and a seafood restaurant. We asked them the simple question: What is this? Here are some of the answers:

PARK: I'd say it's a leaf of some kind.

CRAFTS SHOP: Some artistic design, I guess.

MUSEUM: Oh, let's see. I suppose some form of ancient artifact.

PLASTICS FACTORY: A piece of plastic left over from some production.

SEAFOOD RESTAURANT: Seaweed.

Why did people choose the answers they did? One reason is the CONTEXT in which they were answering. Their surroundings and experiences helped them make certain assumptions — beliefs about what they are describing.

NOW let's try an experiment. Suppose you saw this shape

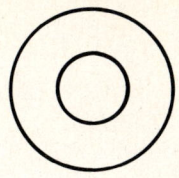

but only the dark outline — none of the details. It is three feet in diameter (the widest distance from one side to the other). What would it look like to you in the following contexts?

on a ship _____

in a garage _____

in a candy store _____

in a gym _____

in a bakery _____

in a fire station _____

in a hospital _____

on a beach _____

See, the context does help determine what you think you see.

Many people learn new words from the meaning of other words in the sentence or paragraph. In other words, they learn from context. Here are some exercises with nonsense words to show you how important context can be.

The following ten words were invented. They don't have *any* meaning in themselves.

greoff	snabutar	screndle	kendelve	anabore
scring	norswick	banafleck	treflic	rostidel

Guess what they mean. Have other people guess what they mean. Be outrageous in your guesses. No inhibitions. Talk about your guesses and write them down.

Notes for Students

Without context, those words can mean anything at all.

Now let's take the first word *greoff* and add some context to surround it — at first just a little:

Context Makes a Difference 39

"The *groeff* stood by the door."

Well, now, you can probably guess a little closer. A greoff is a thing. It's not an action, or a description, or a thought, or a direction.

Let's add a little more:

"The greoff stood by the door, tapping its right front hoof."

Oh, it's an animal.

"The huge, furry greoff stood menacingly by the door, making loud noises, swaying to and fro and tapping its right front hoof on the muddy earth. All the people inside shuddered in fear, awaiting the arrival of the militia, who might be able to slay the dreadful beast and save them from the horror of attack by their seldom-seen enemy from deep in the forest."

Now we get the picture. Let's get out of here!

Now that we've put *greoff* into context, let's do the same with just a sentence about each of the other words. Remember, these words are not recognized English words. But we can give them meaning by giving them context. Notice how these crazy words seem to have meaning in the following sentences.

1. My *snabutar* burned out last night and now I can't listen to my favorite music.
2. Did you *screndle* the ball when she passed it to you or did you hold on to it and make a point?
3. *Kendelve* the grocery list. We only have enough money for peanut butter.
4. Where's my *scring*? I left it here with my tennis racket, balls, sneakers, and towel, and now it's gone.
5. Harry's *norswick* ran away from home two weeks ago and today we found it cold and hungry under the back porch.
6. We sat quietly in the *banafleck* waiting to see the doctor, but he never showed up.
7. Wow! You are the most *treflic* person I've ever known. I've never seen anybody handle a boa constrictor like that before and not show one bit of fear.
8. Did you *anabore* me today at 8:30? I thought I heard something but I wasn't quite awake.
9. Oh, *rostidel, rostidel, rostidel*! That's all I ever hear is *rostidel*! OK, here's five dollars. Go down to the bakery and get a pound of *rostidel*, but be sure they put it in a double bag!

NOW try to guess meanings, answering in this way: _____ probably means _____ because _____. You can condense your answers into the following form, if you like.

Word	Possible Meaning	Reason
snabutar		
screndle		
kendelve		
anabore		
scring		
norswick		
banafleck		
treflic		
rostidel		

What if you guessed WRONG? No problem. In the case of a real word you didn't understand, you could use a dictionary or ask the speaker to define the word. Or reading further might help you find the meaning.

Now here is a good game to show how context aids understanding. Have each member of your group make up a nonsense word and give it a definition, but ask group members not to reveal their definitions. Then ask each to present his or her made-up word and act out the meaning of it for the rest of the group. Whoever guesses the meaning gets the next turn to pantomime (act out without words).

Again, to show that the way you look at something depends on who you are and what your situation is, let's take a look at a particular circumstance:

"*A house is burning out of control!*"

Now you might be inclined to say that EVERYONE would look at that as a BAD thing. But someone might not. In the following chart, list people who might think of the house burning as a good thing and those who could think of it as a bad thing.

The house is burning.

Context Makes a Difference

Good	Bad
_____	_____
_____	_____
_____	_____
_____	_____
_____	_____
_____	_____
_____	_____
_____	_____
_____	_____

In our group we made this list:

Good

A new fireman excited by the experience.

A burglar who had just robbed the house and was glad his fingerprints would be burned off.

The woman who lived there, and was glad to have an excuse to move to another house.

A neighbor who didn't like the architecture of the house because it didn't match the rest of the neighborhood.

Bad

The man who lived there and was sad because he had been writing a book for years and now his manuscript was burning up.

The landlord, because he didn't have it insured for its full value.

Eleven-year-old Amy, who had just finished decorating her room just exactly the way she wanted it.

The grandmother who lived there, because it had been her home for most of her life.

Do this I DON'T CARE exercise to find *several* meanings of the *same* expression.

Event	Response	Thought	Possible Feeling
Someone says, "Do you want to go to a movie or dancing?"	"I don't care."	"It doesn't matter. I like both." (It really doesn't make any difference.)	calm, OK
Someone says, "Do you want to go to a movie or dancing?"	"I don't care."	"No matter what I decide, we'll go where *you* want to go." (I don't have any choice so why even try to decide?)	irritated, disgusted

Thinking Straight and Talking Sense

| Someone says, "Do you want to go to a movie or dancing?" | "I don't care." | "If it doesn't make any difference to you, why should it make any difference to me?" (I really don't want to do either very much.) | Uninterested, bored, turned off |

From here on, fill in the parentheses and the Possible Feeling.

Event	Response	Thought	Possible Feeling
Someone spills soup on your white pants and says, "Oh, I ruined your clothes!"	"I don't care."	"I can get them cleaned easily." ( )	
Someone says, "I think it's going to snow tomorrow."	"I don't care."	"Every time I try to plan some fun outdoors it's ruined by the weather!" ( )	
Someone asks, "Can I use your math book?"	"I don't care."	"I'm not using it now. Why not?" ( )	
Someone says, "You're the slowest person on this team!"	"I don't care."	"I didn't want to be on this team in the first place. If I wanted to, I could go faster." ( )	

Do you agree that your THOUGHTS and FEELINGS are part of the CONTEXT of an *event*?

Context Makes a Difference

8 Smoke in the Sky — Bread on the Table?

NOTES FOR TEACHERS

To understand the principal idea of Rational-Emotive Education — that emotional disturbances and upsets generally come from irrational attitudes and beliefs about oneself, others, and the surrounding world — it is important to understand the concepts of cause and effect. For many — children and adults alike — this is a difficult concept to comprehend. In this lesson we begin with a regional expression to examine cause and effect. You may find it helpful to discuss our example at considerable length. Then ask your group to give similar examples. Suggesting and discussing such examples from the context of many personal experiences will help the group grasp the concepts of cause and effect. A related goal in the following exercise is to encourage a thoughtful examination of the possibilities. Problem-solving, the main theme of Part II, often calls for a willingness to search for the options and the hesitancy to jump to conclusions. This lesson also introduces the concept of skepticism, which we suggest that you encourage and reinforce in your group and in yourself.

Notes for Students

A friend of ours from Lorain, Ohio, tells us there's a popular saying in that town that goes like this:

"When there's smoke in the sky, there's bread on the table."

Does this mean that smoke causes bread to appear on tables?

Or, maybe, that bread somehow causes smoke to be in the sky?

Is it true that every time there is smoke in the sky in

Lorain, Ohio, there is a loaf of bread on every table in the town?

NO!   NO!   NO!

This expression developed from the fact that Lorain is a community with steel pipe production as its main industry.

The steel mills have large towers which give off smoke during the production of pipes.

Smoke in the sky in Lorain suggests that the steel mills are open and the factory workers are employed.

Employment means income or money to buy the necessities for oneself and one's family.

Bread on the table represents food and other necessities for survival.

So, when people are working, they may have enough money to buy food for themselves and their families.

There is, after all, a *relationship* between smoke in the sky and bread on the table, but the popular saying distorts it. Smoke does not cause bread.

Some relationships are much more obvious. Take the knee-jerk reflex. Tap an area directly below the knee and the leg of a reasonably healthy person will kick out.

In this case, tapping the leg causes it to kick.

If most relationships were as simple as this, we would know a lot more than we do.

However, there are really very few such obvious CAUSE-AND-EFFECT RELATIONSHIPS.

Many scientists, detectives, researchers, archaeologists, experimenters, and district attorneys work at discovering what events are related to or cause other events.

How do you know if an event causes another event to occur?

There is no easy answer to this question but there are some clues or suggestions that can help.

If two events occur close together in time and space, possibly they are related to one another. (If you see a person about to swing a banner and a moment later you hear a bell ring from the same direction, there may be a causal relationship.)

If a first event closely resembles a second event, there is a possibility that they are related to each other. (If Dennis Waychik was known to have put a tack on Ms. Gluck's chair during first-period class, and there was a tack on Mr. Wilson's chair during second period class, *and* Dennis was in Mr. Wilson's second-period class, the facts might suggest a causal relationship. Then again, Dennis might have had nothing to do with the tack on Mr. Wil-

Smoke in the Sky — Bread on the Table?

son's chair. Assumptions of causal relationships call for very careful checking.)

If there is a logical or sensible explanation for the relationship of two events, the possibility that they are related becomes greater. (Consider the likelihood of a relationship between smoking and lung cancer.)

If a first event is observed to precede a second event a great many times by a number of different people, there may be a causal relationship. (When many prehistoric people saw the light leaving the sky at sunset, they assumed that the sun was the source of light — that it caused the light.)

If an experimenter creates an event in an experiment to see if a second event occurs repeatedly, then the experiment may demonstrate a causal relationship. (Suppose an experimenter gives one group of monkeys food each time those monkeys figure out a problem on a computer. If they learn how to do that problem better than a group of monkeys that is not given food for doing the same thing — the control group — then there may be a causal relationship between learning and receiving food.)

FOR the following pairs of events rate the possibility (in your opinion) of the *first* event's causing the *second* event to occur. Use the ratings 1 (no chance) to 10 (certainly).

First Event	Second Event	Possibility
John loses car keys	late to work	_____
grandpa gets pain in arm	rain shower begins	_____
student dips paper in liquid	paper turns blue	_____
old woman dies	delivery boy gets rich	_____
man wins lottery	people in movie laugh	_____
phone rings	concentration is disturbed	_____
she grits her teeth	the race is over	_____
Helen spills salt	trips over chair	_____
Joe gets married	Roy gets angry	_____
factory produces pollution	eyes burn	_____

Is there full agreement on the relationship of all the pairs of events?   Yes _____   No _____

Do some relationships seem more causal than others?   Yes _____   No _____

What are the possible explanations for the causal relationships that you rated high?

Notes for Students

We suggest that, although many things may be related, you take care not to assume a cause-effect relationship until you have tested it out.

This kind of carefulness is called SKEPTICISM and it can serve as a valuable trait for people who deal with relationships.

The next time you hear a relationship stated this way . . .

Walking under a ladder causes bad luck.
Eating too much causes overweight.
Money is the cause of all evil.
The problems in the Middle East are caused
by the oil shortage.
Breaking a mirror will lead to seven bad years.
Success in school means success in work.
Not drinking ice water keeps you from growing old.

. . . ask these questions (but bear in mind that even the most positive answers do not necessarily *prove* a relationship in all cases):

• Are there parts of the first event that are contained in the second event?
• Is there a logical or sensible explanation for the relationship?
• Has the relationship between the two events been observed by a number of people on a number of occasions?
• Has an experiment been performed to test the strength of the relationship?

What do the terms in the relationship mean and are they agreed upon by most people?

By asking and answering these questions you are expressing skepticism and enabling yourself to make better choices and decisions about relationships that affect you.

Smoke in the Sky — Bread on the Table?

9 What About Feelings?

NOTES FOR TEACHERS

Rereading and discussing in class "The Fable of Ralph Ram" is a good way to begin this unit.

Notes for Students

We have looked at facts and opinions, conditions and contexts, causes and effects. We have a better idea of what we can be sure of and what is open to interpretation. We have learned in "The Fable of Ralph Ram" that the way we feel about something or someone is not the only view we can take. So what about feelings (which are also called emotions)? Aren't we "supposed" to have them? "I'm *feeling* some way almost all the time," one student said after working through the first lessons in this course. "And now I'm confused. I can't help the way I feel, can I?"

Yes, everyone has feelings. And, yes, you can help the way you feel. That's what this course is about — to help people learn how to train their emotions. People can learn how not to get angry, how not to make themselves feel worthless, how to get what they want some of the time and not to make themselves unhappy when they don't get everything they want. Later units will show how to gain these and similar skills, but the first step is to learn what words and signals express feelings.

WHAT words do you use when you want to describe a feeling? List as many as you can individually on a separate sheet of paper and then put your list together with others to make a master list for the whole class.

Here is one list. Use it as an example.

down	flying	together
tense	angry	groovy
all right	weird	hopeful
crazy	turned on	trusting
ashamed	turned off	bad
hanging in	terrific	embarrassed
happy	excited	afraid
scared	thrilled	mellow
disappointed	hot	hostile
frustrated	sorry	great
in the pits	nervous	silly
fascinated	O.K.	blue
confused	depressed	concerned
messed up	sad	worried
guilty	upset	confident
low	curious	lonely
freaked out	relaxed	high
annoyed	anxious	naughty
in love	faded out	distraught
dynamite	cool	apathetic
wiped out	zonked	in a buzz
arrogant	uptight	funny
cheerful	determined	envious

Here are some projects that can help us look at the variety of feelings people have.

Make a list of some synonyms or near-synonyms for feelings. (Some examples are *emotions*, *moods*, *sentiments*.)

Write down all the different "I feel _____" or "I'm in a _____ mood" statements that you hear others make in one day.

Have someone in your group make a card file of "I feel _____" statements. Have everyone practice going through the cards and acting out each statement. (This will include facial expressions and body motions without talk.)

Have one person go through the file and wordlessly

What About Feelings?

act out each "I feel" statement in front of the rest of the group. See if the group can guess what feeling that person is expressing. (Your guesses can't be right or wrong — that's why they are called guesses. There is not one way to express the same feeling.)

Now take the same "I feel" expressions and show them first only with the eyes. Then only with the hands. Next only with the shoulders. Now only with the lips. Next only with the head. And, finally, only with the index finger.

Choose five "I feel" statements and express them only by using a nonsense sound like "Ba, ba, ba." This will show how much feeling you can convey just by the tone of your voice.

Make a wall chart of all the "I feel _____" statements you have collected. Keep adding to it.

Start a diary of "I feel" or "I felt" statements. At first just write the statements. Don't put down any "becauses."

After you have kept your diary for a day, begin to add clauses that tell *when* you feel a certain way. Leave the "becauses" out. As an example, you might write, "I felt silly when I started writing this diary."

Choose one "I feel" statement (like "I feel happy") and take snapshots of everyone in the group expressing that feeling. Make a wall chart headed I FEEL _____ and attach all of the snapshots to it.

Cut pictures of people out of old magazines and newspapers and paste them onto cards or cardboard. Don't label them. Ask several people to describe what they think they themselves would be feeling if they looked like the people in the pictures. They could say, "This is my picture and I feel _____."

Notes for Students

Remember —

The same "I feel" statement can be shown and said in many different ways.

The same "I feel" expression on different people's faces may mean different things.

You all look sad.

Yeah, I am.

No, I'm just tired.

Nope. I feel great. I'm just thinking something deep.

10 How Events and Thoughts Affect Feelings

NOTES FOR TEACHERS

In the preceding activities, we worked on identifying feelings and the way people express them. Now we are going to see how events and conditions and the way we think about them may produce feelings. We suggest extensive discussions after each of the following activities to make sure that everyone grasps the material. No matter what age group is involved, if people have the idea that their feelings are impossible to change or control, it will be important to give the following exercises an unusual amount of attention and practice. It probably took years to develop the old habits of thinking; changing them will involve some interesting hard work.

Notes for Students

Here are some *circumstances* or *events* that might be associated with some of the feelings we listed in Unit 9. Notice that we have placed an **A** in front of the *event* and a **C** in front of the *feeling*. This is in preparation for a new **A-B-C** idea we will study soon.

1. **(A)** Event — I got an A in English.

    (C) Feeling — I felt **happy.**

2. **(A)** Event — I got ripped off on the way to the bus.

    (C) Feeling — I felt **angry.**

3. **(A)** Event — I heard a noise about 1:00 last night.

    (C) Feeling — I felt **scared.**

4. **(A)** Event — I had to recite a poem in front of the class.

   (C) Feeling — I felt **nervous.**

5. **(A)** Event — I listened to some of my favorite music.

   (C) Feeling — I felt **relaxed.**

Below are six other feelings. Make up an event that might be associated with each of these.

6. **(A)** Event — _____

   (C) Feeling — I felt **disappointed.**

7. **(A)** Event — _____

   (C) Feeling — I felt **embarrassed.**

8. **(A)** Event — _____

   (C) Feeling — I felt **proud.**

9. **(A)** Event — _____

   (C) Feeling — I felt **curious.**

10. **(A)** Event — _____

    (C) Feeling — I felt **hurt.**

11. **(A)** Event — _____

    (C) Feeling — I felt **frustrated.**

• •

Now, read each event given below and then write the feeling *you* might have.

1. My mother came home and told us we weren't moving to the new house. I felt _____.
2. I received my math test back with a grade of 76%. I felt _____.
3. I saw an old man dressed in shabby clothes and he asked me for a dime. I felt _____.
4. The subway doors opened, the crowds of people pushed in, and I was squashed between a tall woman and a short man. I felt _____.
5. The people were yelling, calling my name. There were hundreds of them. I felt _____.

Compare your feelings for each event with other

members of your class. Do you find that there are different feelings for the same event? If your experience is like ours, the answer is "yes." How is this possible?

In each of the examples given above, there is something missing between the Event (which we call A) and the Feeling (which we call C). This "something" (we'll call it B) is really the "cause" of the feeling. Read the examples below and see if you can guess what we will call **B**.

EXAMPLE 1:
A (Event)   I got an A in English.
B (   )   "Now, finally, people will realize how smart I am."
C (Feeling) I felt happy.

EXAMPLE 2:
A (Event)   I got ripped off on my way to the bus.
B (   )   "I must be a real punk for people to treat me that way."
C (Feeling) I felt angry.

Did you get the same answer for both examples? Did you say *belief* or *what you think* about an event? If so, you hit on the answer. The event (**A**) is followed by your belief (**B**) concerning the event, which results in your feeling (**C**).

Any answer that shows one's understanding of the main idea of Rational-Emotive Therapy — that it's people's thoughts or beliefs that cause their feelings to occur — can be used to help explain the relationship between the A's (Events), B's (Beliefs or Thoughts), and C's (Feelings). Answers like "It's what you're thinking" and "It's what people say to themselves" describe B pretty well. "It's what a person is feeling," however, calls for sorting out the difference between thoughts (beliefs) and feelings. Many people find it difficult at first to see the difference between feelings and the self-statements that lead to the feelings. The following material will help point up the difference.

(**A**) I got an A in English, and
(**C**) I felt happy
because
(**B**) I was thinking:

1. I worked hard for that A and I deserve it.
or

2. Now I'll get the attention I want.
   or
3. I think my parents will reward me.
   or
4. I got a higher grade than the boy who's usually tops in the class.
   or
5. That will balance out my C average to a B.
   or
6. I always knew I was smart and this proves it.

At this point go back to the A - C combinations numbered 1 through 5 at the beginning of this unit. For each of the five examples, list in your notebook at least three thoughts or beliefs (B) that you might have had if that event had happened to you. Make the thoughts as different as you can, as long as they seem to fit the feelings described at C.

In the above activity, we kept the event (**A**) and the feelings (**C**) the same while we varied (**B**) to show that several different beliefs might apply. Now let's ask this question: Could *you*, one person, have *different* feelings about the *same* event. Of course you could. If your *thoughts* were different, your *feelings* could change. Let's go back to our opening example: "I got an A in English. I felt happy." Why did you feel happy? Perhaps because you told yourself at B: "I think my parents will reward me." But suppose you had told yourself something else at B — something like: "Now my parents will expect me to get A's in every class." Then you might say: "I got an A in English. I felt sad."

The following activity will help you see how a single event can produce many different beliefs and feelings. We have listed a variety of feelings below. We have also listed five events. For each event (A) select one feeling (C) and, in the space between the event and feeling, write one belief (B) that you think might result in that feeling. Then select another *very different* feeling (C) from the list, and fill in the belief (B) that seems appropriate to produce such a feeling.

Here is the list of feelings, which is followed by an example:

happy, solemn, frustrated, jealous, excited, angry, disgusted, fearful, relieved, nervous, shocked, apathetic, disappointed, scared, curious, proud, upset, ashamed, hurt, relieved, contemptuous, grumpy, wistful, annoyed, anx-

Thinking Straight and Talking Sense

ious, thrilled, disappointed, disturbed, pleased, hopeful, sensuous, perturbed, confused, greedy, self-righteous, satisfied, mellow, apathetic, distraught, arrogant

EXAMPLE:

Event (**A**) - I saw a kid stealing candy in the store.

Now select a word from the list of feelings and put it at **C**.

Then go back and make up a belief that fits at **B**. Suppose you pick the feeling *jealous.* Then you might fill in the belief at **B** to read: I wish I could have that candy.

Now select a very different word from the list of feelings. Suppose you pick *thrilled.* Then you might fill in the belief at **B** to read: If this same guy is the bicycle thief at school, maybe I can do some detective work and get my bike back.

The finished example would look like this:
- **A.** I saw a kid stealing candy in the store.
- **B.** I wish I could have that candy.
- **C.** Jealous

or
- **B.** If this same guy is the bicycle thief at school, maybe I can do some detective work and get my bike back.
- **C.** Thrilled

Now fill in the following blank spaces in the same way. Remember to select the feeling that you want to fill in at **C** *before* you make up the belief that fits at **B**.

- **A.** I heard the news report about the fire at the factory.
- **B.** _____
  _____
- **C.** _____

or
- **B.** _____
  _____
- **C.** _____

- **A.** I didn't get an invitation to Deegee's party.
- **B.** _____
  _____
- **C.** _____

or

How Events and Thoughts Affect Feelings

B. _____
_____

C. _____

A. I sank five out of ten foul shots from the line.
B. _____
_____

C. _____
or
B. _____
_____

C. _____

A. I heard my Uncle Al was coming for dinner.
B. _____
_____

C. _____
or
B. _____
_____

C. _____

A. I decided it would be better to have the letter typed.
B. _____
_____

C. _____
or
B. _____
_____

C. _____

11 Who Causes Your Feelings?

NOTES FOR TEACHERS

This unit requires patient, intensive instruction and application. In the last unit, we began to see how the way we view an event or condition affects our emotional attitude toward the event or condition. This is one of the most important concepts to master in this book, because it is a basic first step toward rational alternatives. Anyone who has ever experienced upsetting emotions (and that covers just about everybody) will find it takes a lot of thought and practice to apply this concept to all areas of living. While many will acknowledge the logic of this concept when it applies to relatively unimportant events, they tend to make an exception with respect to their relationships to people they hold dear as well as their attitude toward great physical peril. In this unit, we show how in these areas, too, the same principle applies.

Notes for Students

Many of us think that other people *make* us feel a certain way. While it's true that others do things that make it easier or more difficult to feel one way or another, *we* are the ones who determine our own feelings. The following activity helps us to see how others don't *make* us feel anything.

Let's begin with a silly expression: "You made me love you. I didn't want to do it." *Not so!* As we stated before, people's own thoughts, beliefs, or attitudes cause their feelings to occur. If you hadn't *wanted* to love a person, then you wouldn't have loved that person.

Does that last statement go against the romantic ideas you've heard for years? It refutes one of many myths that pervade our culture. Let's take another common example: "He made me cry." Translated into behavioral language, we could say: "He did something I didn't like and I thought, 'What a terrible thing to do to me!' and I felt miserable and I cried." That pretty clearly shows that you made yourself cry because of the statement you told yourself, doesn't it?

Is there a way the statement *he made me cry* could make some sense? Perhaps. Let's try this far-fetched translation: "He snuck up on me when I wasn't looking, tied me to the kitchen chair, and began peeling an onion in front of my eyes." That would be a fairly unlikely situation, so let's watch it before we accuse other people or conditions of making us feel the way we do.

• • • • • • • • • • • • • • • • • •

TRY translating the following statements into far-fetched but accurate ones.

He really upsets me.

Translation: _____

_____

She makes me angry.

Translation: _____

_____

My mother makes me feel very guilty.

Translation: _____

_____

I can't go to school because of that teacher.

Translation: _____

_____

Every time I'm with my sister she makes me so depressed I can't eat.

Translation: _____

_____

My friend Geri really makes me laugh.

Translation: _____

_____

You made me love you.

Translation: _____

_____

I can't stand him.

Translation: _____
_____

She makes me feel like a nobody.

Translation: _____
_____

My girlfriend makes me feel like a real man.

Translation: _____
_____

Did any of those statements stump you?

Notes for Students

Now let's go on to the questions raised by major life-and-death events.

Is it possible not to feel terrible if something "terrible" happens to you?

Is it possible not to feel great if something "great" happens to you?

We believe the answer to both questions is: Yes! Here are our reasons:

1. It is not the events that make us feel "great" or "terrible" but our thoughts, and *we can change them.* For example, during crisis situations such as explosions, plane crashes, and mine accidents, instead of saying, "This is terrible. I'm terrified that I'm going to die," many people say to themselves, "I'm not going to panic. I'm going to look at the situation carefully and do what I can to survive."
2. Very often, what appears to be "terrible" or "great" may be less so after we examine it more carefully.

For example: "The house burned down, *but* nobody lived in it at the time." Or: "He just got a new car for his birthday, *but* now that he's twenty-one he doesn't get any more money from the trust fund."

LET'S try this approach with some "good news" and "bad news." Complete each sentence below by describing a condition or set of conditions which could explain why you are glad and *not upset* about the stated fact.

Who Causes Your Feelings?

1. I came in *last* in the race and I'm *glad* because _____.
2. I got a *cold* and I'm really *glad* because _____.
3. I have no money, nowhere to go, and nothing to do this evening and I'm *glad* because _____.
4. The utilities company turned off our electricity and gas and I'm *glad* because _____.
5. My best friend moved a thousand miles away and I'm *glad* because _____.
6. It's pouring outside and we're home alone. Our TV is broken, someone stole our radio, our record player doesn't work, the library is closed, all our games are in school, the phone is out of order, the newspaper company is on strike, the dog chewed up all of our magazines, we've read every one of our books, and I'm really *glad* because _____.

Now complete each sentence below by describing a condition or set of conditions which could explain why you feel sad and *not pleased* about the stated fact.

1. I received the highest grade in my geography test and I'm *sad* because _____.
2. I won the grand prize in the sweepstake contest and I'm *sad* because _____.
3. I was asked to go to the party with the most popular boy (or girl) in the school and I'm *sad* because _____.
4. I earn a very good income, own two expensive cars, have a twelve-room mansion and I'm *sad* because _____.
5. My picture and a very nice story about me appeared in the city newspaper today and I'm *sad* because _____.
6. My sister just had a baby and I'm *sad* because _____.

Is it a little clearer now that you have the ability to control what you feel?

Thinking Straight and Talking Sense

12 Getting Rational

NOTES FOR TEACHERS

The activities in this section introduce the skills of challenging, disputing, and articulating rational alternatives to irrationality. While we expect that this book will be used mainly in schools, *this book is not just for students.* We strongly believe, and have received much information to support our belief, that the teachers involved with the uses of this book can derive great benefits from it. If such adults will *do* the activities themselves, *look* at their work and their interpersonal relations — indeed, their *lives* — in the context suggested here, *risk* creatively and responsibly, and *think* about what these concepts mean to them, the effectiveness and value of this curriculum will increase for everyone involved.

Notes for Students

What can you do about it when you've got a feeling you want to get rid of? This activity introduces a technique for changing negative feelings that will be used many times later in this book.

Crazy! Upset! Distraught! Furious!

These are words expressing strong emotions that most people are better off without. It would be difficult to imagine anyone *wanting* to feel these ways. These strong feelings would probably not help most people live satisfactorily. Because of this we call such feelings (and the beliefs that produce them) irrational.

Irrational means without clear thinking or good sense.

Let's take some very obvious irrational examples to show what we mean:

— believing that the only way to deal with people you disagree with is to kill them.
— believing that you must be the very best in *every* task, game, event, or activity that you participate in.
— believing that other people *should* act exactly as you do or as you want them to.
— believing that, if you make a mistake, you are an unfit human being and do not deserve to live.
— believing that you are *the* most important person in the world and completely disregarding or abusing the rights and feelings of others.
— believing that *no* other human being has *ever* experienced (even to a slight degree) the kinds of events, thoughts, and feelings that you have and therefore can *never* understand you nor you, them.

What other irrational examples can you think of?

No doubt you will find some differences of opinion in your group. Because beliefs and feelings happen inside a person, it is sometimes difficult for people to agree on what a specific belief or feeling is.

Who knows your beliefs and feelings best? *You do!* Anyone else can just guess at or try to understand them. Nevertheless, as you learn to make your beliefs and feelings clearer to yourself, you may very well learn to communicate them better to others.

The quite obvious irrational examples are easy. Probably most people would agree that they are irrational. But there are many other ideas, values, and feelings people have that would not be so easy to classify as irrational or rational. Some beliefs and emotions in one context would be more rational than the same beliefs and emotions in another context.

For example, worrying about getting the right answer to a question makes more sense if being wrong would cost your life than it does in a school classroom.

How do you know if your beliefs, feelings, and behaviors are irrational in any particular context?

Sometimes the words we use to express our beliefs can help us decide whether these beliefs are rational or irrational. The following words are often associated with self-defeating, irrational beliefs:

Words of Exaggeration
awful   horrible
terrible   bummed out
wiped out   devastating
dreadful

Absolutes or Unrealistic Demands

must	should
ought	got to
need	insist
have to	

• •

WRITE one or more examples of irrational beliefs using each of the words above.

Although care in using these words, and an awareness of their association with irrational thinking, is useful, don't go overboard about it. People have their own very individual styles of thinking and expressing themselves, and the same word may mean altogether different things to different people. The words used above are some of *our* suggestions based on *our* thinking and experience. It may help you create your own lists of words and phrases that represent crazy, mixed-up thinking for *you*.

Here are some of the criteria (measures or tests) that we have used to check irrationality in ourselves. We have put them in question form. Apply them to a few of your beliefs or feelings. A *no* answer to any question may indicate irrationality about your beliefs, feelings, and behaviors.

- Do they aid in your personal survival?
- Do they promote a clearer understanding of your life?
- Do they help you fulfill your desires?
- Do they lead to a state of happiness?
- Do they make sense to you?

NOTES FOR TEACHERS

It is advisable to proceed slowly with this material. Use a lot of class-related examples — a typical day in the lives of most people has its share of irrationality. Ask for personal experiences or share some of your own. For each probable irrational belief, go back to the preceding questions. Does it meet any of the criteria? (It need not meet them all.) As you discover instances of irrational beliefs, you can introduce the following material on challenging and disputing.

Getting Rational

**ACTIVITY
ACTIVITY
ACTIVITY**

ONCE you have decided, either by yourself or with the help of others, that some of your actions or emotions and the beliefs that produce them are irrational, here is a way to bring about some change. It is a technique for challenging and disputing any irrational belief, and it involves asking yourself a series of questions. As you ask yourself the questions, answer as honestly as you can, and use our examples to help you analyze your answers.

1. *What is the irrational belief?* Define it. State it in the way you're saying it to yourself.

    EXAMPLE: If I don't make the school basketball team this term, it means I'm no good and I'll never be able to play organized basketball again.

2. *How much do you want to give up this belief? How willing are you to work at the challenging and disputing?* Answer on a scale of 1 (very little) to 10 (very much). The closer your honest answer is to 10 the better chance you will have of giving up this irrational belief.

3. *What proof is there to show that the belief is false (irrational)?*

    EXAMPLE:

    a. Even if you don't make the school team, it does not mean you're no good (overall as a person) and it may or may not mean that you are not skilled in basketball.

    b. If you don't make the school team this year, you may make it another year.

    c. If you're not accepted in this particular situation, there is no good reason to generalize to all situations. You could become a valuable member of a team for a community center or a boys' or girls' club or a Y.

    d. Even if you're very poorly skilled in basketball, there is no reason that you can't play the game at your own pace and level and enjoy it. If you care about it, you probably can improve.

    e. There are many examples of people who have failed in some task or endeavor, only to go on to success in the same area at a later time. A number of professional basketball players did not get on their high school team.

4. *Does any evidence exist of the truth of this belief?*

    EXAMPLE: No. Not making a school basketball team, especially if you worked hard at it, is very disappointing. That kind of rejection can lead to all kinds of negative feelings — but in no way does it prove you're no good. Because that implies that you are never good in anything you do, never have been, and never will be and Step 3 above shows this to be false.

5. *Can I rationally support this belief?* We believe that, after you carefully progress from Steps 1 through 4 above, your answer to this question will be *NO!*

NOTES FOR TEACHERS

Since a great deal of this material involves didactic instruction, it is essential to make every effort to engage the interest and involvement of the students. This can be accomplished through a variety of teaching approaches, with particular emphasis on each individual student and his or her problems. We urge that you not rush or push this material. Spread it out over a number of periods, days, or even weeks.

Notes for Students

We often call the challenging and Disputing of irrational Beliefs, the D's. In Unit 10 we introduced the A's and B's and C's. If we put them all together now, this is what we have:

the A's —— *the Activating Event.* What happens — usually the thing (event) that starts off a new feeling.

the B's —— *the thoughts and Beliefs about what happens.* Usually includes an evaluation (good or bad) of what happens.

the C's —— *the Consequence.* The reaction to what happens, in feeling and behavior.

the D's —— *the Disputing and challenging of the beliefs.* Asking questions about the beliefs.

There is one more step in this alphabetical approach of changing and dealing with uncomfortable negative feelings, and that step is

the E's —— *the Cognitive Effect* (CE) or outcome of disputing and challenging. The answers to the questions and the new feelings and new behaviors (BE) that come from working through the A, B, C, D, and E's.

Sometimes we use a chart to work through the A, B, C, D, and E's. Here's what it looks like.

Getting Rational

C		
A		
B	1. 2.	
D	1. 2.	
CE	1. 2.	
BE		

Questions — rows B, D
Answers — rows CE, BE

Let's go through the chart step by step.

1. Indicate your reaction to the entire situation.

C	I'm feeling disgusted with myself.

2. Describe the event that you're feeling, whatever way you're feeling, about:

A	After working with a tutor for three weeks and studying very hard for the last two days, I get a 51% on the math test.

3. Write your beliefs about the events. Include the irrational ones. Those are the ones that need challenging.

B	1. This is the end of the road. 2. I can't stand working so hard and failing. 3. I'm not smart enough for school. I'd be better off in Calaveras County training frogs.

4. Dispute and challenge the irrational beliefs by questioning and answering questions.

Questions

D	1. A statement like, "This is the end of the road," doesn't mean much in reality. What's a truer description of the situation? 2. Why can't I stand it? 3. What proof is there that I'm not smart enough for school?

Thinking Straight and Talking Sense

Answers

CE
1. It's a crummy situation to be in. I may get a very low or failing grade in math. But it's not the end of my life.
2. I'm still breathing. I can still eat, have friends, enjoy games, and do other things that I did before. Obviously, I can stand it, as difficult as it is. I'd be better off thinking how I can improve things than complaining about how bad they are.
3. Getting a 51% on the test does not mean I'm not smart enough for school. There are many things a person can learn in school. It does not even mean I'm not smart enough for math. It might help to look over the situation carefully and decide if there is more I could do to improve my grade. As far as training frogs goes, that might be the best move of all.

5. Write the outcome of the disputing and challenging on your feelings and your behavior.

BE I feel less disgusted with myself. Mostly I'm just disappointed. I'm going to speak to my math teacher and try to get some pointers. Then I'm going to try to get a new math tutor. I'm also going to start studying way before the next test so as to avoid a last-minute rush. And the thought about moving to Calaveras County in the future really turns me on. Maybe I could train frogs and teach math on the side.

Whenever you experience self-destructive emotions (like anger or guilt or frustration or jealousy or any other unpleasant feelings), go back over this material and apply it to your immediate problem. As you keep working at it and practicing, it can help you avoid a lot of unhappiness and get more enjoyment and satisfaction out of your life.

13 Your Credo

NOTES FOR TEACHERS

This is the last unit in Part I. It moves on from the techniques for developing rational alternatives as opposed to irrational and self-defeating behavior to an inquiry into basic individual attitudes and personal credo. Self-knowledge — awareness of one's beliefs — helps the individual get control of his or her thoughts and feelings. It stimulates intellectual growth and challenges the imagination when the student tests his or her personal credo against new information and differing beliefs. The activities in this unit offer an opportunity for lively group discussions and projects which can expand horizons of interest for teachers as well as students. This unit merits a number of class sessions, which can be adapted to the special problems of the individual, the school, and the community, as well as to world issues. Its application can extend to many courses — science, literature, history, and so on. It also offers an excellent practical basis for reinforcing the material learned in the previous unit.

Notes for Students

All of us have things we believe. We hold on to some of our beliefs for years, others keep changing, but one thing is for sure, our beliefs have a lot of influence on our behavior. This activity helps us to look at what we believe and find out how our beliefs influence what we do. It asks the question, "Can we learn something about the ways we behave by learning more about what we believe?"

Credo

In REE we think that what we believe has a lot to do with what we think and feel about events.

WHAT DO YOU BELIEVE?

Check the items below that you agree with.

I believe in democracy! ☐

I believe in fair play. ☐

I believe it's a hard life, but it's harder if you don't try to better yourself. ☐

I believe in a supreme being. ☐

I believe for every drop of rain that falls a flower grows. ☐

I believe in the scientific method. ☐

I believe in myself. ☐

I believe in living each day as if it were my last. ☐

Notes for Students

While we're in the process of gathering information about ourselves, let's review the idea that there are many different areas of our lives:

ACADEMIC (school and intellectual stuff)
ATHLETIC AND PHYSICAL (related to our bodies)
DAILY LIVING (survival skills)
INTERPERSONAL (dealing with other people)
   and
ATTITUDES AND BELIEFS

This last area is sometimes forgotten because, unlike the ACADEMIC, which can be seen in school results, ATHLETIC AND PHYSICAL, which can be seen in games and sport, DAILY LIVING, which is seen in tasks and chores we do,
   and
INTERPERSONAL, which is seen in relationships with friends, relatives, and others,
   ATTITUDES AND BELIEFS are impossible to see.

What are attitudes and beliefs?
In the way we're using the words, attitudes and beliefs are the rules you use to live by. When you put all of your attitudes and beliefs together, they form your PERSONAL CREDO.

Where do they come from?
We're not completely sure of that answer. Like thoughts, they're a combination of experience and what we do with the experience in our minds.

How do they differ from thoughts?
A thought is about one particular experience.

EXAMPLE
When I was at Barbara Ventura's house last Thursday night, I thought to myself, "What expensive furniture she has!" Beliefs or attitudes are usually about a whole set or type of experiences.

EXAMPLE
Every time I'm with people who have a lot of money I get annoyed because there are so many poor people in the world.

Why is it important to gather information on our beliefs and attitudes?
Because it is these very attitudes and beliefs that influence our thinking and lead to our feelings of sadness, happiness, anger, and the like.

When we're aware of our beliefs, we have a much better chance of being in control of how we think and feel, if that's what we choose to do. Also, by studying beliefs and attitudes, we can learn a lot about facts and theories, people and places. A student we know, while working on these activities, made a list of beliefs that were important to him. One of them was:

"Nobody has the right to take anybody else's life."

He discussed this with other people in his class and there was some disagreement.

"If someone killed my mother, I'd go out and get them."

"What about in self-defense?"

"Suppose someone asked you to kill him or her?"

He still stuck with his belief. A couple of days later someone brought an article to school about capital punishment. He read the article and became very interested. Before the school year was over, using this one belief as his springboard, the young man —

— wrote four letters — to a congressperson, an author who had been in prison, a newspaper, and the American Civil Liberties Union

— read a book about life on death row and a few articles about capital punishment

— visited, with his teacher and other members of his class, a prison in the city in which he lived

— added many new words to his vocabulary

— watched a five-part television news series on euthanasia

— telephoned the local Planned Parenthood group in his community and arranged for a speaker to come and talk to his class

— and moderated a panel discussion on capital punishment

• •

HERE are some activities that we have used with students and with teachers to help gather information about our beliefs and attitudes ... our PERSONAL CREDO.

We suggest that all of these activities be done individually first and then shared with others, in pairs, small groups, or the whole class.

Before each of the following phrases or statements read the words, *Do I believe* ... Answer each question with a YES or NO response. This may be difficult for you to do with some phrases or statements, but *force* yourself to pick the one response that you're closest to.

1. that I am a good person? _____
2. that I have control over other people? _____
3. that the United States of America is the best country in the world? _____
4. in God? _____
5. there's no hope with dope? _____
6. that I will live to be at least sixty-five years old? _____
7. that if I break a mirror I'll be unlucky? _____
8. in love at first sight? _____
9. that I must do well in school? _____
10. that blondes have more fun? _____
11. that I have control over myself? _____
12. that life is very important? _____
13. in ESP? _____
14. that I know myself very well? _____
15. in Santa Claus? _____
16. that what the world needs now is love? _____
17. that people can make changes in their lives? _____
18. that there are evil people in this world? _____
19. that childhood is the best time of life? _____
20. that some people are born losers? _____
21. that I will be famous one day? _____
22. that it's important to take care of my body by exercising and eating right? _____

Your Credo

23. that most kids and their parents aren't really friends? _____
24. that if a man and woman have more than two children, the earth will become overpopulated? _____
25. in happy endings? _____
26. that a lot of people who are lazy get what they want by luck? _____
27. that fun is necessary? _____
28. that I could survive as a prisoner in a concentration camp? _____
29. that taking risks is a big mistake? _____
30. in different strokes for different folks? _____
31. that people who sell things on commercials on TV believe in the product they sell? _____
32. that medical doctors deserve a lot of admiration and respect? _____
33. that if I were in great danger I could kill another person? _____
34. that there is a heaven and a hell? _____
35. that I have a chance to become President of the United States? _____
36. in making fun of other people? _____
37. that smoking cigarettes is an unhealthful and dangerous thing to do? _____
38. that people who get good grades in school deserve them? _____
39. in abortion? _____
40. that people must earn their rights? _____
41. that older people should be treated with respect? _____
42. that if I wish for something very hard it'll come true? _____
43. in socialized medicine? _____
44. that people who have a lot of money are greedy? _____
45. that I'm going to get married when I get older? _____
46. that poor people in the United States could improve their conditions if they really wanted to? _____
47. that I am loved? _____
48. that if I were stranded on a desert island I could survive? _____
49. that movie stars are happy? _____
50. that nuclear power is a good way to provide energy? _____

TAKE ME TO YOUR LEADER(S)

Directions: A Martian lands near your house, knocks on your door and, when you open it, says, "Look, I've only got a week's vacation. I've got to be back on Mars by the 4th of Uranus. I'd like a guided tour of Earth — the deluxe package. Here is a list of the kinds of things I want to do and see and learn. I want you to help me fill it out. I know nothing about the people or places on Earth so I'm leaving it all up to you. Transportation is no problem. I can zoom you anywhere on Earth in less than one minute.

Here it is:

Monday — Visit the five most important famous people in the world.

1. _____
2. _____
3. _____
4. _____
5. _____

Tuesday — Read the best book written by an Earthling or Earthlings.

Name of Book _____

Author (if known) _____

Wednesday — See three of the most impressive things Earthlings have built.

1. _____
2. _____
3. _____

Thursday — Day Off (I'm visiting my cousin Ernie in Oxnard, California).

Friday — Meet the five most important people you know personally.

1. _____
2. _____
3. _____
4. _____
5. _____

Your Credo

Saturday — Learn the language. Teach me six words in your language — three words that you think are important to know and three that are words you don't like.

Positive   *Negative*

1. _____   1. _____

2. _____   2. _____

3. _____   3. _____

Sunday — Share CREDOS. In order of importance list the three beliefs you most cherish.

1. _____

2. _____

3. _____

Remember we said a CREDO is like a set of rules? Well, can you imagine playing a game like basketball without understanding the rules?

You'd step out of bounds with the ball and lose possession of it.

You'd bounce the ball with two hands and it would go over to the other team.

You'd touch someone on the arm as he or she was dribbling, and a violation would be called against you.

You'd shoot the ball for the wrong basket and score two points for the other team.

It might be a very frustrating experience.

Knowing your own set of beliefs and attitudes can help you to see which of your beliefs are —

— helping you to think irrationally
— and feel negatively
— and, therefore, preventing you from getting what you want.

PART 2
Problem-Solving Skills

A Word About Problems and How to Solve Them

YOUNG people and the adults who work with them in classrooms spend a great deal of time together. Sometimes, for some of us, it seems to be too much time, and we'd rather not be there. But there we are! What can we do about it? How can we, individually and together, make it a better experience? We think one way is by learning, sharing, and experimenting with skills that can be used in problem-solving. We see problems as (1) any kind of unsolved question or situation and (2) those particular questions and situations that are related to strong negative emotions.

An example of the first kind of problem might be an assignment to write a report for social studies. Until the assignment is complete, the problem is unsolved. All the activities and information that lead to the finishing of that report are part of problem-solving. There may be some general negative reaction, but it will not be directed against the problem itself in any intense way.

The second kind of problem could be the same assignment accompanied by strong feelings of anxiety, frustration, or anger. In this instance, any activity and information that would reduce the negative feelings would also be part of problem-solving.

Rational-Emotive Education is an approach that recognizes the existence of both kinds of problems and the skills to deal with them. REE has four equally important emphases. The first is a theoretical or philosophic background. It includes the basic assumptions presented in the introductory pages of this book. It is the foundation for the second part of REE, the methodology — how to do it. If beliefs create feelings, it follows that feelings can be changed by changing beliefs.

The third aspect of REE is the people using the approach. Questioning, clarifying, and gathering information about the internal and external events, thoughts, and feelings in a person's life define this part. Ours is an interactional curriculum. No two people will find the experience of REE exactly alike. Each person can bring his or her unique events, beliefs, and feelings to interact with the activities, lessons, and methods of Rational-Emotive Education.

Finally, the fourth emphasis is on applying REE theory and methods to the facts of one's life.

When all parts of REE are utilized, it becomes a prime problem-solving tool for students and adults. The activities and lessons in this unit present opportunities for people to integrate the basic skills presented in Part I with specific ways of recognizing and working out the many types of problems that are created and encountered in the process of getting educated and growing up.

Several activities in Part II demonstrate a variety of unconventional ways of looking at problem-solving. Their purpose is to demonstrate and encourage alternative, creative, or lateral ways of thinking. Many problems in school are of the kind described at the beginning of this discussion. A child can't do a certain type of math operation, a teacher doesn't know what to plan for the next day, a group of students can't decide on which activities to participate in during independent study. Such experiences strung together often encourage irrational thinking, which leads to the second kind of problem: "Not only can't I do this but it's terrible and awful that I should even have to try." Believing as we do that the best cure is prevention, we urge the reinforcement of creative, individual approaches to questions and situations.

The remaining activities in Part II concern those problems that are no longer interesting challenges but have become (through our irrational thinking) disturbances in our lives. The book culminates with a plan for the future, using many of the concepts and methods of REE to influence our future behavior, beliefs, and emotions.

Pretest

Notes for TEACHERS and STUDENTS

The concepts introduced in Part II are: **1.** changing feelings by changing thoughts **2.** "winning" and "losing," "failing" and "succeeding," "errors" and "corrections" **3.** sharing strengths **4.** creative problem-solving **5.** resourcefulness **6.** assessing the possible outcomes of an action **7.** aggressiveness, assertiveness, passiveness **8.** challenging irrational beliefs **9.** insults **10.** goal-setting

Pretest for Students

1. Are you stupid if you answer a question incorrectly?

    Yes _____ No _____ Why or why not? _____
    _____

2. Are you strong or good because you win or succeed?

    Yes _____ No _____ Why or why not? _____
    _____

3. What is the worst that would probably happen if you lost a contest or failed a test? _____
    _____

4. How do you feel when you share something that someone appreciates? _____
    _____

5. Is there always one right way to do something?

    Yes _____ No _____

6. Do you agree with this statement? "The more skills and resources you have the better able you are to solve a problem."

    Yes _____ No _____

7. Can you always predict how something is going to turn out before you do it? Yes _____ No _____

8. Do you agree with this statement? "It is better to have risked (responsibly) and lost than never to have risked at all?"

    Yes _____ No _____

9. Do you always feel the same about the same event?

    Yes _____ No _____ Why or why not? _____
    _____

10. Do you always communicate clearly to another person what you want that person to see or hear? Yes _____ No _____

    Why or why not? _____
    _____

11. Read the following responses and mark them AS (for assertive) or AG (for aggressive) or P (for passive):

    Someone says in a loud, forceful voice, "Get over here right now!" and gets the following responses:

    a. _____ OK, if you insist.

    b. _____ Forget it! *You* come here! I'm not moving!

    c. _____ Why do you want me to come there? I'd be glad to do it if I understood.

    d. _____ Well, I guess you're the boss, so I will. (Thinking, "Boy, I really don't want to!")

    e. _____ Come there? Would you mind asking a little less forcefully? I'd be glad to cooperate, but I really don't like to be ordered around.

    f. _____ No! I wouldn't move an inch for a creep like you!

12. Do you agree with the following statement? "One goal of interpersonal communication is to get what I want without taking away anything that the other person does not want to give willingly." Yes _____ No _____

13. Is it possible always to predict what another person is going to think of what you do? Yes _____ No _____

14. Is a person "bad" because that person makes mistakes?

    Yes _____ No _____

15. Does everyone make mistakes? Yes _____ No _____
16. If you are feeling miserable, is there anything you can do about it? Yes _____ No _____ If yes, what? _____
17. Who is the "best" person in the world? _____
18. When you win something, do you win everything? Yes _____ No _____ When you lose something, do you lose everything? Yes _____ No _____
19. What would you do if someone said to you, "You're ugly"?
_____

What are some other choices? _____
_____
_____
_____

20. Do you have any control over your future? Yes _____ No _____
How do you know this? _____
_____
_____

Key to Answers to Questions in Pretest

1. No.
2. No.
3. This is open to your opinion. However, you would probably not die, nor would the world come to an end.
4. This answer will be different for nearly everybody.
5. No.
6. When you are asked whether you agree or disagree with an answer, whatever truthful answer you give would respond correctly to the question. As to the statement in Question 6, REE proposes that this is true.
7. No.
8. The answer to Question 6 applies here.
9. Most people will probably answer No, because they often *think* differently about the same event.
10. Most people will probably answer No.
11. a. P___   c. AS___   e. AS___
    b. AG___ d. P___   f. AG___
12. The answer to Question 6 applies here.
13. No.
14. No.
15. Yes.
16. Yes.
17. No one.
18. No. No.
19. When you are asked what you would do in a situation, whatever truthful answer you give would respond correctly to the question. As to the statement in Question 19, REE proposes that you think something like
    "Well, that's just one opinion."
    or
    "What does that mean?"
    or
    "Can you prove it?"
    and respond in an assertive but not aggressive or passive way, if you are going to respond. Another choice is to ignore.
20. Yes, because you have the power to think rationally, clarify your life patterns, set goals, and take risks.

14 Looking at Your Skills

NOTES FOR TEACHERS

This activity is an aid to general problem-solving. It can benefit people of almost every age, and it is a good practice to use it for periodic checkups. There is a special note suggesting how teachers can share their interests and build closer ties with class members. The rewards for everyone concerned are rich when a teacher succeeds in transforming a "routine" teaching job into an exciting, stimulating classroom experience.

Notes for Students

All of us *behave*. We do things. They tell a lot about us. This activity helps you to get a clearer look at *what* you do and in what patterns. It may also help you do more of the things you like to do. It asks the question, "How can I use what helps me in one part of my life to help me in another part of my life?"

THINK back over the past month. What did you do outside of school that you enjoyed most? List those activities in your notebook. (EXAMPLES: rode a bike around the city, cooked Spanish rice, organized a photo album, made a collage, read a detective story, gave a friend a massage, found out about my ethnic background, went dancing.) Be specific and list as many as you can. Head your list: **List I - Out of School.**

Now make a similar list on another page of things *in school* that you enjoyed most. Head your list: **List II - In School.**

1. Can you see any *themes* or categories in Lists I and II? (To help you discover themes or categories, answer the following questions with respect to each of your activities.)
    (a) Did you think of the activity or did someone else suggest it?
    (b) Does it involve other people or is it done alone?
    (c) Does it involve materials?
    (d) Does it cost anything or is it free?
    (e) Would you like to continue doing the activity or was it a one-shot episode?
    (f) Was the activity based on new learning or skills you already had?
    (g) Was the activity generally acceptable to others or would it likely be seen as unacceptable?
    (h) Do lots of other people engage in this activity or is it unusual?
2. How do the two lists compare in length?
3. Are there many similar items?
    (a) If so, what are they?
    (b) What does that mean?
    (c) Would you like there to be more?
    (d) Would you like there to be fewer?

Now go back and sum up everything you have examined in this unit. Having identified some themes in your life, do you begin to see some useful patterns? Ask yourself this question: "If I can see clearly what helps me in one part of my life, can I figure out how to use it to help me in other parts of my life?"

Notes for Students

Some people at this point might see an advantage in developing more of a parallel between their lives out of school and in school. Couldn't those things you already do and really enjoy be content for some of your curriculum — a sharing of your life away from school with the students you teach? Try some of these suggestions:

1. Bring some meaningful things from home and put them in your school room — items like photographs, plants, and trophies.

Looking at Your Skills

2. Invite a friend or relative to visit you at school and learn or participate in an activity.
3. Set aside a daily or weekly period of a half hour for independent activity in your classroom, and you participate by bringing in an independent activity for yourself.
4. Include a personal interest as a legitimate activity in your regular teaching schedule (for example, photography, gourmet cooking, yoga, needlepoint, psychotherapy).
5. Organize a weekly afternoon of mini-courses offered optionally by teachers and students in the areas of their interests and skills.
6. List all your interests on a chart and put it on a wall of your classroom. At the bottom write, "This could be a place for us to grow, too."
7. Build a life line of some significant moments in your personal history. Display it in the classroom. These can vary: peak moments, sorrows, educational development, interpersonal relationships, good times, and the like.

15 Learning from a Master Nasty List

NOTES FOR TEACHERS

Many people make themselves miserable because they don't like some people and some people don't like them. Some individuals even go so far as to believe that they are completely worthless if a few (or many) other people don't like them. The activities in this unit will have applications almost everywhere — at home, on the job, in the classroom, on the playground, in social situations. As classroom squabbles arise, you will have an excellent opportunity to review this unit again and again with your group.

Notes for Students

Most of us dislike some others and are disliked by some of them. Many of us spend a lot of time liking and disliking and thinking about whether we're liked or disliked. This activity helps us look at whom we dislike and what effect our dislike has on them. *It asks the question, "How important is it that everyone likes me and thinks well of all the things I do?"*

Does this sound familiar? "I hate her. She makes me sick to my stomach. She's so disgusting, I can't stand her. I don't ever want to see her again. I hope she. . . ." How many times have you heard someone say something like that? Have you ever felt that way yourself? In REE we don't believe that kind of thinking helps you to feel better or to get what you want. Let's work on developing a more productive type of thinking.

WRITE down the names of five people (friends, relatives, acquaintances — whether kids or adults) whom you have great contempt for, or of whom you disapprove strongly, or whom you have unresolved conflicts with, or whose actions turn you off. In short, list people you *just don't like.* Update your list next week. You may use the same five people each week or replace some or all of the people as new conflicts and interpersonal problems occur in your life.

The following forms are set up for a two-week project. If you want to continue your nasty lists for a longer time than that, you can set up similar forms in your notebook.

NASTY LIST

	Week 1	Week 2
1	_____	_____
2	_____	_____
3	_____	_____
4	_____	_____
5	_____	_____

Write each person's name on the MASTER NASTY LIST and indicate your feeling and main thought about each person.

MASTER NASTY LIST

	Person	Feeling About Person	Thought About Person
1	_____	_____	_____
2	_____	_____	_____
3	_____	_____	_____
4	_____	_____	_____
5	_____	_____	_____
6	_____	_____	_____
7	_____	_____	_____
8	_____	_____	_____
9	_____	_____	_____
10	_____	_____	_____

Notes for Students

Now let's look at the differences between SUBJECTIVE and OBJECTIVE evaluations. SUBJECTIVE evaluations are individual or personal opinions. They are just one way of looking at something that happened, and they may be wrong. OBJECTIVE evaluations may be made by one person, but can be agreed upon by many. They are concerned with action that can be observed (seen, heard, touched, smelled, etc.) — facts.

By using OBJECTIVE rather than SUBJECTIVE evaluation you run fewer chances of making mistakes. This doesn't mean that you'll never make a mistake (research scientists who use very objective methods often make mistakes) or that it will be horrible if you do mess up (you'll be just about the same person that you were before the mistake).

READ each of the following statements. For each one ask yourself, "Does the statement describe behavior that can be seen or heard or felt or touched or smelled, and agreed upon by most people?" If the answer is YES, check the column marked OBJECTIVE. If the answer is NO or NOT SURE, check the SUBJECTIVE column.

		Objective	Subjective
1.	I blew his mind.	_____	_____
2.	He realized what an idiot he was.	_____	_____
3.	Patty sat down and cried.	_____	_____
4.	Mario felt so badly he wanted to cry.	_____	_____
5.	He felt smaller than a bug playing handball on the curb.	_____	_____
6.	She kicked Esther on her leg.	_____	_____
7.	I know that remark about his mother really hurt him.	_____	_____

8. When Carl thought about me he got very scared. _____ _____

9. The fight really upset Jonathan. _____ _____

10. Ronnie told Ms. Wilkes to go "!*?%!" _____ _____

11. The two kids from the projects ran down Willis Avenue to 141st Street and then cut over to St. Ann's. _____ _____

12. He was so annoyed about the weekend that he almost punched the wall. _____ _____

13. All the fighting in the room got to him and he started acting crazy. _____ _____

From our point of view, recognizing BEHAVIORS that can be seen, only 3, 6, 10, and 11 are objective evaluations of what could be observed. All the others are subjective opinions.

Now, go back to the Nasty List and estimate the amount of influence your dislike has on the lives of those on it. In your estimate of the amount of influence your dislike has on the person on your MASTER NASTY LIST, look for OBJECTIVE examples. Did the person tell you that your dislike was upsetting to him or her or did you just *assume* it? As a result of your hostility, did the target person bump into a pole while walking home, or did you just assume that person was worried about you?

Rate the degree of your influence from 1 (few or no objective examples) to 10 (a great many objective examples). We can call this estimate a "guesstimate" because you really don't know the exact answer to this. It's just a guess.

MASTER NASTY LIST

Name	Weeks on List	Influence
1. _____	_____	_____
2. _____	_____	_____
3. _____	_____	_____
4. _____	_____	_____
5. _____	_____	_____
6. _____	_____	_____
7. _____	_____	_____
8. _____	_____	_____
9. _____	_____	_____
10. _____	_____	_____

Ask yourself these questions when your MASTER NASTY LIST is completed:

Did my opinion and negative feelings about these people MAKE them any less happy?

Did my disapproval STOP them from getting what they want?

Did any big changes happen in the lives of the people on my list clearly because of my disapproval?

Did the number of weeks that a person was on my list make any difference as far as my influence on that person was concerned?

The answers to these questions will probably be No or Not Much, since your feelings in and of themselves cannot change the behavior of another person. Ask yourself now, "HOW IMPORTANT IS IT THAT EVERYONE LIKE *ME* AND THINK WELL OF *ALL* THE THINGS *I* DO?"

In Unit 10 we introduced the A, B, C, D, and E's. Try completing the following A-B-C-D-E chart on being disliked. If necessary, go back and review this material in Units 10 and 12.

Learning from a Master Nasty List

	A	You overhear a group of kids in school saying that they really dislike you. Some of the kids in the group are your so-called friends.
	B	**1.** I'll never be able to face any of those kids again. **2.** I hate this school, this neighborhood, and this city. **3.** This is the worst day of my life. I want to die.
Feelings	**C**	
Questions	**D**	**1.** What forces could stop you from facing these kids again if you wanted to? **2.** What does the event you experienced have to do with the school, the neighborhood, or the city? **3.** Even if this day is extremely bad because of what happened, does it require you to die?
Answers	**CE**	**1.** **2.** **3.**
Emotions and Behaviors and Future Plans	**BE**	**1.** **2.** **3.**

Have all the members of your group share their charts. This will give you lots of ideas.

Thinking Straight and Talking Sense

16 Test-Making Can Be Fun

NOTES FOR TEACHERS

This unit can help defuse anxiety concerning tests by putting the construction of tests in the student's hands. (This is a method you may want to carry over to many subject areas.) It also challenges the use of the terms *smart* and *stupid* — very often irrational labels that many students and teachers hold about others and themselves. The first activity can encourage and legitimize the study of one's life as a valid subject in school. And it may provide people who are turned off, shy, or bored with a new motivation to learn.

MAKE up a test on some area of knowledge that is very familiar to you. Create it from your own experience. Start with yourself. You can have easy and hard questions, fill-ins, multiple choice, matching, and essay questions. Test your friends, relatives, and classmates. Here's an example:

MID-TERM EXAM ON FRANK MONAGHAN

1. Frank's nickname is:
   Big ____   Irish ____   Frankie ____   Red ____
2. Frank lives in the section of Brooklyn called _____.
3. The girl Frank is going with is Ellen.
   True ____ False ____
4. Fill in the correct answer in Column A with one of the items in Column B.

Column A		Column B
best friend	_____	pizza
hobby	_____	artichokes
favorite food	_____	William
brother's name	_____	seven
age	_____	Tony
apartment number	_____	Sean
middle name	_____	bowling
favorite sport	_____	chess
least-liked food	_____	nineteen
total of digits in phone number	_____	thirty-four
father's name	_____	hamburgers
		Harry
		P. J.
		stamp collecting
		thirty
		asparagus
		drawing
		cartoons
		cars
		Donna

5. Write an essay of about a hundred words describing the main differences in Frank's life in Ireland and in the United States.

Now that you have seen an example of the kind of test we mean, begin to think about the subject for your own test. What do you know a lot about? The test does not have to be on facts about your life or someone you know. It can be a general information test on a variety of subjects you've learned. Like a lot of people, you probably know some facts about many different things.

Some people who have done this activity have used the following topics for their tests: their family, people who live in their building, the stores in their neighborhood, baseball players, the real names of some famous people, movie stars, math puzzles, food, tropical fish, their own ethnic background, states in the United States, cartoon drawing, gerbils, opera, New Orleans, dancing, presidents of the United States, race cars, scientific experiments, riddles, taking care of young babies.

Here's how to work out your test:

Step 1. Decide how many people will be involved in the project. (It could be partners, small groups, or large classes.) _____

Step 2. Decide what topic or topics your test will cover. _____

Step 3. Decide how many questions you will have. (Consider a five-question or a ten-question test.) _____

Step 4. How will the test be graded? (It's a good idea for the person who makes it up to grade it and use a simple number-correct and number-incorrect system.) _____
_____

Step 5. What are your questions? (Use as many different types of questions as you can.)

1. _____
_____
2. _____
_____
3. _____
_____
4. _____
_____
5. _____
_____
6. _____
_____
7. _____
_____
8. _____
_____
9. _____
_____
10. _____
_____

Step 6. Now look over your questions and decide how you can teach the information that will provide the answers to the questions without revealing the actual questions. Suppose, for example, one of your questions is: Which of the following movies was Robert De Niro in? *Superman, The Sting, The Deer Hunter, Star Wars, The Godfather.* Then before you present that question, teach your partner, group, or class that Robert Di Niro has acted in a number of movies and that some of them were *Taxi Driver, New York, New York, The Deer Hunter, Bang the Drum Slowly.*

Make notes on how you're going to handle your presentation. You can talk the whole thing. You can write on the board. You can display pictures or charts. You can show slides. You can act things out. You can bring equipment. You can demonstrate how something works.

Practice your presentation before giving it. Do it in front of a mirror or with a friend or relative. Write out your notes on 3 × 5 cards or a sheet of paper.

Step 7. Decide how long your presentation will take. Find out if you will be limited to a certain period of time. Practice your presentation once or twice to make sure it will fit your time frame. If it's too long, it may become dull. If it's too short, add more background material.

Presentation will take _____ minutes.

Step 8. After the presentation, when will the test be given? (When this is done with partners, both people may first give their presentations, and then they can both exchange tests and do them simultaneously. With groups, the test may be given immediately following each presentation.) _____

_____

Step 9. Grade the test. (See Step 4.)

Step 10. Consider what this grade means. The following activity will help you examine and perhaps revise your attitude toward grades.

The purpose of this next activity is to demonstrate that self-labels such as "smart" or "stupid" are usually created by people's own beliefs about what they do (and sometimes what they are told about themselves). It will show that these labels are changeable.

How do you feel when you tell yourself sentences like these? "I'm smart." "I'm stupid." Generally you tend to give yourself a good (positive) feeling or a bad (negative) feeling when you make statements like that, don't you?

For each of the following statements about you, write a thought that would lead to a positive and one that would lead to a negative feeling. Think of both feelings as not extreme. Note this example:

STATEMENT: You're a real fool for doing something like that.

THOUGHT   POSITIVE FEELING I'm so glad he disagreed with me. I thought the matter through and saw where I could handle the situation better next time. Meanwhile, it's no great catastrophe.

THOUGHT   NEGATIVE FEELING Criticized again! I can't stand it much longer. Now I'll never try to do something like that again!

STATEMENT: I'm so proud of you. You're the smartest student in my class.

THOUGHT   POSITIVE FEELING _____
_____

THOUGHT   NEGATIVE FEELING _____
_____

STATEMENT: It's about time you start showing people all the potential you have. You're very lazy.

THOUGHT   POSITIVE FEELING _____
_____

THOUGHT   NEGATIVE FEELING _____
_____

STATEMENT: You're so important to me. I don't know what I'd do without you.

THOUGHT   POSITIVE FEELING _____
_____

THOUGHT   NEGATIVE FEELING _____
_____

STATEMENT: You're just no good. You've never been worth anything. I have no use for you.

THOUGHT   POSITIVE FEELING _____

_____

_____

THOUGHT   NEGATIVE FEELING _____

_____

_____

Now that you have shown that you can have either a positive or a negative response to the same statement, do you see how it is possible to change your feelings about grades? Of course, it is best to avoid making any statement like "You are dumb" to yourself or to anyone else. It is better simply to say, "Edward answered three out of five questions correctly in that test." That is a true statement about the results of a specific test taken at a specific time about a specific subject or subjects. It does not in any way *rate* the individual; it simply describes the performance in a specific instance.

Let's go back now to Step 10, in which you are asked to consider what the grade means that you gave your partner in the test you made up. What do you think it means if your partner answered all the questions incorrectly, or answered some correctly and some incorrectly, or answered all of them correctly?

☐ I'll tell you what it means if (s)he gets a zero. It means (s)he's stupid!

☐ I think there are other possible explanations.

☐ It could mean that (s)he didn't study the facts you taught. . .

☐ . . . or that (s)he just doesn't know some facts that you know — but probably knows other information that you may not. . .

☐ . . . or (s)he purposely put down answers you would mark incorrect even though (s)he knew which were the correct answers. . .

☐ . . . or that (s)he and you do not agree on what are the correct answers. . .

☐ . . . or that (s)he has very poor academic skills, often gets zeros on tests, didn't understand the information even though it was presented clearly but is still the same person (s)he was before the test, not stupid or smart. . .

☐ . . . in fact, the description of your partner (or yourself) as stupid is pretty stupid itself (that is, it doesn't make sense) because it means (s)he is always stupid about all things.

O.K., now let's change the circumstances a little. Your partner has made up a general information test and has taught you such facts as the most popular flavor of Baskin-Robbins ice cream, her or his favorite book, the number of giraffes in the San Diego Zoo, Pele's real name, and the annual salary of the Chief Justice of the Supreme Court. You take the test and answer all the questions correctly.

I guess that means I'm pretty smart. Right?

Are there other possible explanations? _____

_____

_____

_____

Challenge that belief!

Now that you have prepared your own test and have given the necessary information to someone to prepare for the test and then have graded the results of the test, do you see tests and grading a little differently from the way you did before? Tests can be a good deal of fun. That's why the quiz shows on television are so popular. You may find it a great help in learning new material to make up your own tests. The following *supplemental activity* covers many different types of questions you can use in making up a test. The more types you know about, the more varied the form of your test can be. Generally, the greater the variety, the greater the interest.

Here are some types of questions. For each one look for the answer (a) in your head, or (b) with a friend, or (c) in a book, or (d) by asking someone, or (e) in a newspaper or magazine, or (f) by calling someone up, or (g) from your parents, or (h) by guessing. Then make up your own example of that type of question, based on information that you have.

1. **TRUE-FALSE**

   ONE EXAMPLE: There are 26 letters in the Greek alphabet.

   TRUE ____   FALSE ____

   ANOTHER EXAMPLE: If Jenny Smith, age 28, never gave birth to a baby, she can't be a mother.

   TRUE ____   FALSE ____

   YOUR EXAMPLE: _____

   _____

   TRUE ____   FALSE ____

2. **YES-NO**

   ONE EXAMPLE: Is Henry Kissinger your gym teacher?

   YES ____   NO ____

   YOUR EXAMPLE: _____

   _____

   YES ____   NO ____

3. **FILL-IN**

   ONE EXAMPLE: _____ was the twenty-first president of the United States.

   ANOTHER EXAMPLE: Red and _____ mixed together yield orange.

   YOUR EXAMPLE: _____

   _____

4. **LISTING**

   ONE EXAMPLE: Name nine cities in the state of Colorado.

   1. _____ 2. _____ 3. _____
   4. _____ 5. _____ 6. _____
   7. _____ 8. _____ 9. _____

   ANOTHER EXAMPLE: List three ways to get from your house to school.

   1. _____
   2. _____
   3. _____

   YOUR EXAMPLE: _____

   _____

   _____

5. MULTIPLE CHOICE

ONE EXAMPLE: Which of the following is a Japanese food?
☐ Pork Lo Mein   ☐ Kajihara
☐ Tempura   ☐ Phnom Penh

ANOTHER EXAMPLE: Harold is an art
☐ museum   ☐ treasure
☐ studio   ☐ teacher

YOUR EXAMPLE: _____
_____
_____

6. MATCHING

ONE EXAMPLE: Match the items in Column A with appropriate ones in Column B.

A	B
lunch	numbers
music	cucumbers
English	rhythm
math	rhyme

YOUR EXAMPLE: _____
_____
_____

7. SEQUENCE

ONE EXAMPLE: What is the next number in this series?

18, 10, 6, 4, ____

ANOTHER EXAMPLE: Put the following events in order: went home, ate lunch, went to the rest room, went to math class, woke up

1. _____   2. _____   3. _____
4. _____   5. _____

YOUR EXAMPLE: _____
_____
_____

8. ANALOGY

ONE EXAMPLE: Kareem Abdul-Jabbar is to basketball
in the same way as Bjorn Borg is to
skating   polo   lacrosse   tennis

YOUR EXAMPLE: _____
_____
_____

Test-Making Can Be Fun

9. PUZZLE
ONE EXAMPLE: If Marie is two years older than Lusila, who is one half as old as Jack's bowling average, which is ten times Eva's dress size, which is one hundred and one less than the average temperature for Badwater, California, for July, which is fifty one more than the number of words in this question, how old is Marie? _____

YOUR EXAMPLE: _____
_____
_____

10. INFORMATION:
ONE EXAMPLE: What is triakaidekaphobia? _____

ANOTHER EXAMPLE: Who wrote the book *The Catcher in the Rye*? _____
STILL ANOTHER: What is the Spanish word for the English name Steven? _____
YOUR EXAMPLE: _____
_____

11. ESSAY
ONE EXAMPLE: Write a three-sentence paragraph on "Why Miss Tate Likes Teaching."
ANOTHER EXAMPLE: Write a one-page essay on the major causes of the American Revolution.
YOUR EXAMPLE: _____
_____

12. INFERENCE
ONE EXAMPLE: Since Bill chose to live in New York City, he probably likes
☐ mountain climbing ☐ the Yankees
☐ surfing   ☐ lobster fishing
ANOTHER EXAMPLE: Since Rosa's parents are from Puerto Rico, she probably often eats
☐ arroz con pollo   ☐ mousaka   ☐ coq au vin
☐ blintzes   ☐ goulash
YOUR EXAMPLE: _____
_____
_____

17 Tournaments and Contests

NOTES FOR TEACHERS

You will find it helpful to go back and review the previous material on the A-B-C's (Units 10, 12, and 15) before working on the A-B-C-D-E chart.

Notes for Students

Can you enjoy games and contests, try to do your best, and still not have crazy, irrational thoughts about the importance of winning and losing? We don't say that it's easy, especially when you hear things like

Winning isn't everything. It's the only thing!
Let's go out there and "kill" the other team!
That guy is a real loser!

but we believe that it is possible.

Like everything else, it takes practice to learn to enjoy competing and to be able to take winning or losing in your stride. It helps to work in lots of areas of competition, especially when some of them are really offbeat. Some actual tournaments that were held in one school during a school year were: Jacks (with fancies), Thumb Wrestling, Free-Throw Shooting, Chess, Garbage-Pail Basketball, Staring (to get another person to laugh), Jump Rope, Marbles, Baseball Card Toss, One-Legged Balancing, Pretzel-Eating, Backgammon, Standing Broad Jump, Identifying Landmark Locations.

Step 1. Select a skill that you think you're very good at. Use as your only basis for selection the safety and practicality of doing this in school. Otherwise, the more outrageous, the better. (In one school, a FAST-TALKING CONTEST was developed by a student who normally spoke about two hundred words a minute.) _____
_____
_____

Step 2. Describe the skill involved in clear behavioral terms. What do you have to *do*? (For example, thumb wrestling is a game where two people grasp right hands such that. . . .) _____
_____
_____
_____
_____

Step 3. Describe *all* the rules for the tournament. This step involves a lot of preparation. Think over the contest carefully. How many people can be in it? Are there any time limits? What has to be accomplished to win? Will there be any judges? Who? After you make up the rules, it will be a good idea to check them out with other people to get their suggestions and advice before you make up a final set. _____
_____
_____
_____
_____

(Use your notebook if you need more space for your rules.)

Step 4. If this will be a multi-round tournament (for example, four pairs of people play games of chess; the four winners go on to the next round, where two players are eliminated; and the final pair play for the championship), draw a tournament elimination chart for your skill.

Here are the rules, description, and chart for one tournament:

FAST-TALKING TOURNAMENT

Description Talk as fast as you can, while still speaking clearly.

Chart

Round 1	Round 2	Round 3	Champion
Miriam vs. Randy	_____		
Tawana vs. Grace	_____	_____	
Thomas vs. Frank	_____	_____	_____
Ramon vs. Debbie	_____		

Rules

In each round the participants are given a topic to discuss and a time limit of one minute. The topics are:

Round 1 - *All the People I Know*
Round 2 - *What I Did Today from the Moment I Woke Up Till Now*
Round 3 - *A Description of What I Look Like*

The participants continue talking on the topic for a full minute. A panel of judges (made up of the teacher and two students who are not in the contest) listen to the talks and rate each participant from 1 (low) to 10 (high) on both speed and clarity. The scorecards could look like this:

	Speed	*Clarity*	*Total*
Miriam	_____	_____	_____
Randy	_____	_____	_____

The person with the highest total wins that match. In case of a tie, the match is played over with a different topic.

Tournaments and Contests 103

Step 5. Everyone in the group or class receives information about all of the tournaments. The participants may provide the information in writing or they may verbally describe their tournament to the rest of the group. Along with the information everyone gets a copy of the following Contest Questionnaire.

THE CONTEST QUESTIONNAIRE

Listen to or read the description and rules for each tournament. In each case estimate on a 1 (low) to 10 (high) scale what your chances are of winning. This is nothing more than an educated guess. Asking yourself these questions may help you:

    Do I have any experience with this particular skill?
    How have I performed on this skill in the recent past?
    Have I participated in related kinds of activities?
    How interested am I in participating in this contest?
    What is my competition like in this tournament?

Only the results of the contests will show how accurate your guesses were.

In your notebook list the contests and the ratings you estimate for yourself. Set it up like this:

Name of Contest   *Estimated Rating*

_____   _____

Now answer the following questions:

Are all the ratings the same? Yes _____ No _____

Are there any tournaments or contests that you think you might win (10 rating)? _____

_____

Are there any tournaments in which you think you wouldn't get beyond the first round? _____

_____

What does the fact that you have different ratings mean? _____

_____

Can you be GOOD in everything? _____

Can you be BAD in everything? _____

What can you say to yourself the next time you do poorly or "fail" at some activity? _____

_____

_____

_____

_____

What can you say to yourself the next time you do well in some activity? _____

_____

_____

_____

_____

Study the following A-B-C-D-E chart carefully and answer the questions about it. (To review the A-B-C concept, see Units 10 and 12.)

A	After paying ten dollars to enter a community center-sponsored chess tournament, having very high expectations of success, and telling almost everyone you know about it, you are eliminated in the first contest by a kid three years younger than you.
B	1. I'm no good as a chess player and I guess I never was. 2. Not only am I a lousy chess player but I'm an idiot for having told everyone about it. This is a terrible situation.
C	I feel lousy every time I think about it, and I don't go up to the community center any more.
Questions D	1. Where does *one* chess match define a player as either good or bad? 2. Why does losing a chess match make you an idiot and this situation terrible?

Tournaments and Contests

Answers **CE**
1. Nowhere! Better to assess your skill as a chess player on a more objective basis — perhaps by your winning percentage of time with a variety of opponents.
2. It doesn't. Even if you shot off your mouth, the worst that can happen is that others may think you're an idiot. And even if that happens, which is unlikely, it doesn't make you an idiot. Losing a chess match can be disappointing, frustrating, unfortunate, or even a good learning experience, but it's not horrible.

BE
I feel disappointed at losing (I think I could have done better) and particularly at talking so much about it before it happened. I'm going back to the community center and try to improve my game.

1. What is the disputing question for Belief 1? _____

2. Write a different E for this chart where the person continues to have irrational beliefs. _____

3. What if the person who defeated you in this chess match was a new player — would that mean that you're a terrible chess player?
Yes ____ No ____
Could it mean that you're a terrible person? ____
Why did you answer question 3 as you did? ____

Thinking Straight and Talking Sense

18 Advertising Your Talents

NOTES FOR TEACHERS

People — especially young people — tend to underestimate their abilities, and this activity offers them a fine opportunity to discover their unique skills and talents. It proposes aggressive advertising and marketing and involves groups in pleasurable activity that is excellent preparation for the commercial world.

Notes for Students

What if you could trade yourself? What qualities do you have that others would want? What roles do you play best? What skills do you have that others might find useful?

Pick your most tradable quality or talent. Choose any category — academic, artistic, athletic, general knowledge, relationships, survival — and create an ad to reach your buyers. Here are some samples:

Looking for a good friend? Try Ginger. She listens and helps you out and doesn't bug you when you don't want her to. Call _____.

Parents, Teachers — Now available in a 78-pound package —
LARRY
a cooperative kid to have around

Jacks, Yo-Yos, Jump Ropes, Marbles — Tina does them all and she can teach you!

Having trouble finding your way around the neighborhood? Want a good guide? Danny knows all the paths, fences, walls, secret hiding places, and alleys around.

If you're looking for someone to keep you up on the Top 10 — Rhythm and Blues, Soul, Rock, Country and Western — titles and lyrics — come to Joanne. There's not a song she doesn't know.

Stuck with a question and don't know where to look for the answer? About to give up? Billy knows how to use an encyclopedia, atlas, almanac, dictionary, thesaurus, *Guinness Book of World Records*, and many other reference materials. Look him up — he'll get the information fast.

Your friend Dotty ... knows Karate — she can teach you!

The illustrations above are just some of the ideas that came out of one class. The idea was to focus on something —
    — we like
    — we think we do well
    — we'd like to share
This "something" is not what we ARE — it's just something we HAVE. Try it!

• •

WRITE the thing about yourself you are going to advertise: _____

_____

    Now write, design, and illustrate your ad.
    Communicate your message to the rest of the group. (Our class put up posters, sent flyers, and made public announcements.)
    Answer these questions:
    What do you think of your special thing you are "selling" to other people? _____

_____

    How do you feel about it? _____

Does having it make you a good person? _____

What does having this special thing mean? _____
_____

What would it mean if you didn't have it? _____
_____

Check the statements you agree with:

_____ There are some things I do well.

_____ I don't do everything well.

_____ When I do something well, I feel good.

_____ When I don't do something well, I feel rotten.

If you checked the last statement, we have a question to ask you: Why do you feel rotten when you don't do something well? Is it because you are thinking:

"I'm no good."

"They'll laugh at me and I couldn't stand that!"

"I'll never be able to do that!"

"I hate not being able to do something!"

When we found out that some kids we worked with were telling themselves statements like that, we challenged them to change that thinking. Here's the plan we came up with. It may work for you.

PLAN A TRADE WEEK

First, decide what you want to trade. Here are some examples from our group:

Ginger planned just to sit and listen to people's problems.

Tina planned to teach some techniques for jacks.

Danny drew a map of the neighborhood with all the special routes and places.

Billy planned to teach people how to look up things in reference works.

Dotty planned a presentation on karate.

Carlos decided to teach disco roller-skating.

After the members of your group have selected their specialties to trade, schedule the next three weeks this way:

FIRST WEEK:
1. Advertise.
2. Take a half an hour a day to plan a presentation on your "thing." Get the information you need. Prepare

your material and presentation so the people who "buy" from you may find it fun or informative or both.

SECOND WEEK:

1. Each student fills out cards with the following information:

   My name _____

   What trade item I want _____
   _____

   Person offering trade item I want _____
   _____

TEACHERS Make sure each student has at least one "buyer." If need be, ask one of the usually more cooperative students to "buy" from another who hasn't gotten any response.

2. The teacher and a small student committee make up a schedule and post it on the bulletin board. It might look something like this:

"Seller"	Trade Item	"Buyers"	Time
Larry	How to Cooperate	Jerome, Evelyn	Monday 10:30-10:45
Joanne	Popular Song Lyrics	Darren, Tina, Fay, Valerie, Ramon	Monday 10:30-10:45
Sarah	Caring for Cats	Mr. Dwyer, Paul	Monday 10:45-11:00
Malcolm	Pitching Pennies	Maxine, Eugene, Carol, Derek, Joe, Laverne, Billy	Monday 10:45-11:00

Thinking Straight and Talking Sense

THIRD WEEK:
1. This is TRADE WEEK. Trading will go on every day from 10:30 to 11:30 (or whatever hour you choose).
2. People who are not trading at the time will do independent work.
3. By the end of the week everyone has participated at least twice — once "selling" and once "buying."
4. At the end of the project they answer these questions:

What did I "sell"? _____

_____

What do I think about it? _____

_____

How do I feel about it? _____

_____

Do I want to change my thought and feeling? _____

If so, what can I do? _____

_____

(One thing you can do is use the five steps — A - B - C - D - E — for challenging irrational beliefs. See Units 10, 12, and 17.)

Advertising Your Talents

19 Guessing

NOTES FOR TEACHERS

This activity works through the implications of the adage, "Nothing ventured, nothing gained." It deals particularly with the value of being unafraid to *guess* now and then. It is especially important for people who are afraid to risk being wrong or afraid they will sound silly if they make a mistake. Such people generally appear to know less than they actually know, since they will not speak up unless they are absolutely sure of the answer. That attitude rules out speculating and hypothesizing and imagining — important aspects of the creative process. This unit opens up many possibilities for group discussions of various kinds of risks and the relative benefits of risk-taking in different situations. It points out the difference between risks that can merely cause inconvenience or embarrassment and those that may be life-threatening or have serious consequences. Make sure you draw out the ordinarily less vocal members of the group and encourage them to discuss their personal experiences. It will be helpful to discuss the occasional value of preceding an outright guess with phrases like "My best guess is" or "This is just a hypothesis." And there is also a good opportunity for learning to say matter-of-factly and gracefully, "I was mistaken about that, wasn't I?"

Notes for Students

Sometimes we're right, sometimes we're wrong, sometimes it's hard to tell. Often we're afraid to be wrong because we believe we'll be "bad" if we are. So we avoid taking risks. This activity can help you learn to risk a thoughtful guess. It suggests an answer to the question: Is making a mistake such a terrible thing?

Consider these statements:

"If I'm not all right, I'm all wrong."
"I'm afraid to guess because I might get it wrong."
"I stay quiet so I don't make a mistake."
"I couldn't take it if I goofed."

How many times have you said something like that or heard someone else speak that way? Does it make sense? The fact is that people all over the world fouled up yesterday and — did you notice? — the Earth is still rotating today.

This doesn't mean that there aren't serious errors. There *are*. BUT MOST ERRORS ARE NOT SERIOUS.

It also doesn't mean that it's not a good idea to try to correct errors. Often it *is*. BUT the universe, the Earth, the Western Hemisphere, the United States, your state, your city, your neighborhood, your school, your family PROBABLY didn't fall apart, grind to a halt, or explode simply because you —

— misspelled rhinoceros
— made an error in multiplying 37 × 43
— dialed a wrong number
  or
— mistook someone for someone else

Mistakes are usually INCONVENIENT, A HASSLE, A PAIN, but they are seldom more than that.

• •

THE following exercise can help you feel less sensitive to being wrong. Start with this list of questions. Very few people can answer them correctly, so it is ridiculous to expect correct answers from yourself. Nevertheless, write an answer to *each* question here or in your notebook. Don't know the answer? Then GUESS!

1. Who is the premier of Finland? _____
2. What does an average chickadee egg weigh? ____
3. What is the name of the main street in Chillicothe, Ohio? _____
4. How do you say "peace" in Urdu? _____
5. What is the boiling point of turpentine? ____

Guessing

6. In what year was Warsaw, Poland, founded? _____
7. What is the monetary unit of Upper Volta? _____
8. What is the distance between Neptune and Uranus? _____
9. How many pages are in the telephone directory of Moose Jaw, Saskatchewan? _____
10. How many kilowatts of electricity does the average family in Brisbane, Australia, use daily? _____
11. What is the area in square meters of the Volkswagen plant in Wolfsburg, Germany? _____
12. What was the Somrong-Sen? _____
13. What is the phone number of the police station in Guadalajara, Mexico? _____
14. How high is the tallest building in Albania? _____
15. Do they sell Skippy Peanut Butter in Java? _____
16. What day is Barbara Walters' birthday? _____
17. What is the highest temperature ever recorded in Tierra del Fuego? _____
18. Where is the Tuloma River? _____
19. What is the daily charge for a semi-private room at Mt. Sinai Hospital in Cleveland, Ohio? _____
20. What city's zip code is 27514? _____

Now that you have recorded your best guesses, take the questions home and ask several other people to GUESS the answers.

Bring all those answers back to class. Then take an hour of class time in which your whole group will do research in the dictionary, encyclopedia, almanac, and atlas. Write letters and make phone calls, if you need to, in order to get the *correct* answers. How many of your group and the people you asked at home got *any* answers right?

Hold a group discussion about how you felt toward all your wrong guesses.

Notes for Students

After completing the above activity, a good many people reach the following conclusions:
- There are some questions that have an answer but few people know it.
- It may be more useful to know how to find the information you need when you need it than to cram your head full of miscellaneous bits of knowledge.
- Guessing is not a terrible thing.

Of course, there are some situations in which guessing would be foolish or dangerous. Would you guess the following?
- The way from New York to Buffalo if you were already on the road?
- Whether the thing you were about to eat was a mushroom or a toadstool?
- Whether the smoke you smelled was an inside or an outside fire?
- Whether the date of your friend's party was the 19th or the 26th?

Probably you would want to double check to make sure you had the right answers to questions like that. But there are times when you would be willing to guess, aren't there? If you guessed "wrong," how would you feel?

20 Finding Tools for Change

NOTES FOR TEACHERS

This activity presents an exciting program that can involve your group in the community. It can be used to stimulate interest in social studies, history, and government. And it offers useful training for future jobs. Like many of the other activities in Part II, it promotes the discovery of new talents and abilities. Many students who have not been attracted to more academic studies become enthusiastic about this project.

Notes for Students

Often when we want to make some changes in our lives we delay our progress because we think we don't have the "right" tools to use. Sometimes they're there, but we just don't see them. This unit helps us identify the tools for change that we might use in moving toward a goal. The activity proposed here may help you see that you can learn a lot by *doing* instead of just waiting for something to happen.

There are many ways to help yourself and your community if you really look for them. One resourceful woman used to say, "We were better off when we were poor." She explained that, when people couldn't *buy* their solutions, they made use of what they had and often they got by. We're not suggesting that we all become poor, but we *are* suggesting that there may be more *resources* available to us than we imagine.

Foxfire is a series of books by a group of students in Georgia who went out into their community and discovered the treasures that were there.

"Youth Tutoring Youth" is a program in which older kids help younger kids in school activities.

"Operation Survival" was a program launched by school students of New York City to help the city through its financial crisis.

The resource is often there — recognizing it and getting to it is the problem. It's a funny thing, but people in big cities are often *less* active than people in smaller places because they just don't know how to find their way to the many resources that surround them.

• •

ONE of the things that Rational-Emotive Education is all about is SOLVING (or at least trying to solve) your problems by THINKING. So here's a challenge. Why don't you and your class do yourselves *and* your community a big favor by discovering the resources that are there and writing a guide to them for everyone to use?

One school we know of has published a *Community Resources Guide* and has sold hundreds of them at $1.00 a copy. The people in the area have a tool they never had before, and the students have a whole cluster of benefits. They have a good deal more information than they had *plus* confidence in their ability to discover resources *plus* money for projects they otherwise would not have had.

We'll share with you the plan they used.
1. They decided the categories in which they wanted to find resources and discussed where they thought they could find them. They completed the following chart:

Finding Tools for Change

WHERE TO FIND THE RESOURCES

Category	Library	Yellow Pages	Interviews	Newspaper	Chamber of Commerce	United Way	Mailed Questionnaire
Recreation	___	___	___	___	___	___	___
Sports	___	___	___	___	___	___	___
After-School Programs	___	___	___	___	___	___	___
Tutoring	___	___	___	___	___	___	___
Emergencies	___	___	___	___	___	___	___
Music	___	___	___	___	___	___	___
Art	___	___	___	___	___	___	___
Drama	___	___	___	___	___	___	___
Dance	___	___	___	___	___	___	___
Crafts	___	___	___	___	___	___	___
Entertainment	___	___	___	___	___	___	___
History	___	___	___	___	___	___	___
Food	___	___	___	___	___	___	___
Legal Aid	___	___	___	___	___	___	___
Religion	___	___	___	___	___	___	___
Health	___	___	___	___	___	___	___
Employment	___	___	___	___	___	___	___
Unusual Learning Opportunities	___	___	___	___	___	___	___
Interesting People	___	___	___	___	___	___	___

2. They assigned research tasks to each student who participated in the project. This is the way they set up the assignments:

COMMUNITY RESOURCES PROJECT

Student's Name _____

Category _____

Sources of Information _____

_____

3. All the researchers worked during "Resources" period and recorded their information on this form:

COMMUNITY RESOURCES PROJECT

Category _____

Resource _____

Address _____

Telephone _____

Person Contacted _____

Services _____

Kind of People Served _____

Hours Open _____

4. They filed information on sources by category. (The group got so involved that they advertised in the local newspaper, went door to door, and appeared on television, asking people to help identify local resources. Of course, there were hassles, disorganization, and confusion along the way. But the project moved ahead.)
5. After five weeks they pulled the information together in usable form, put it on Ditto masters, and illustrated it. Three weeks later they had a 78-page guide ready to distribute and sell.

The *Community Resources Guide* reopened opportunities for community involvement for many skilled people in the area.

"This guide is the best thing ever happened to me," said a man who has lived in the community all his life.

"I learned more in that eight weeks than I would have all year without this project," said a participant.

So, what does this project have to do with Rational-Emotive Education?

Here's what some of the students concluded:

"Kids — I guess most people — can do a lot of things they don't think they can do."

"You don't have to do a great job to do a good job."

"Sometimes the solution's right under your nose."

"You learn a lot by doing and not just waiting for something to happen."

All of those conclusions fit right into the objectives of REE. Couldn't those attitudes help you get more of what you want?

Finding Tools for Change

21 The Case Against Trying

NOTES FOR TEACHERS

This unit goes further with the idea of taking risks, setting goals and seeing them through, and sometimes dealing with ridicule or an unsuccessful outcome. Offering people the opportunity to be active and resilient can help them gain useful tools for handling work and social situations all the rest of their lives. Make sure that each individual gets fully involved in this activity.

Notes for Students

Sometimes we want to do something and we begin it but never finish it. It seems like too much effort, and our goal looks too far away. We begin to believe we can't do it. This activity helps us set goals and carry through. It asks, "Isn't it better to risk failure than to take no steps and believe you are safe?"

According to Webster's Dictionary, the word TRY has about five definitions. One of the most popular of these is "to make an attempt" as in "I'm TRYing to do my homework" or "I'll TRY to fix the bike."

Other meanings of TRY use such words as "examine," "investigate," "test the limit."

It seems that the popular version is more watered down or weaker than the others.

Whether or not the common use of TRY did come from the other uses is not important.

It does seem that TRYING is often used in a negative or excuse-making sense — so much so that, in some cases, listening to someone tell how (s)he is trying is indeed a TRYING experience.

One student spent almost a year in a reading class, *not doing any work* and telling anyone who would listen how he was really TRYING, but no one was helping him, the teacher was no good, the work was too easy for him, and the other kids were stupid.

Finally, the teacher did something which showed him how little he was really DOING. She pointed to a pencil near his chair and said, "I bet you can't TRY to pick that pencil up."

He replied, "Sure I can."

As he bent over and reached for the pencil, she yelled, "No! TRY to pick it up."

He sat back in surprise.

She then said in a softer voice, "Try to pick the pencil up."

He bent over again and touched the pencil, and she bellowed, "No! TRY to pick it up."

He turned to her and said, "But I *am* trying."

And she responded, "No, you're not. You're DOING it."

How often do you set a goal for yourself but don't think about how you're going to get to that goal?

What have you been trying to do recently?

Is it clearly set in your mind?

Do you know the steps you're going to take to reach your goal?

• •

HERE are some ideas about DOING things to get to your goal that one group of students presented. They were interested in reducing some of the confusion in a very large social studies cluster class in a junior high school. We believe these ideas can also be used individually to DO something about personal goals.

What do you want to do? What is your goal? _____

_____

_____

Is it clear in your mind? Yes ___ No ___

How will you know when you've reached your goal?

_____

_____

_____

Is it something you can do alone or does it require others? If so, whom? _____
_____

What is the fantastic best result that could come about? Go really far out, the more outrageous the better. (One of our friends from the junior high school came up with, "God will come down on earth and shake our hands.") _____
_____

What is the fantastic worst result that could come about? Again, go to the extreme. (EXAMPLE: "All of the students will be expelled from school and sent to a juvenile detention facility.") _____
_____

Now set your sights more realistically. What is the possible best outcome? (EXAMPLE: "We will make some good changes in at least the cluster group.") _____
_____

What is the possible worst? (EXAMPLE: "No one will care what the outcome is and I'll see this as a waste of time.") _____
_____

Tell some people that you know what your goal is. ("I want to pilot an airplane.") Then ask each one for a single suggestion of something to DO that's related to your goal. ("Visit the store on Horace Harding Expressway that sells hang gliders." "Call my friend Barbara. She's a stewardess for Pan Am." "Go to the library and take out a book on commercial piloting.") Write all the suggestions here or in your notebook and get started DOING them.

_____
_____
_____
_____

Here are some supplemental activities you can use to flex your DOING muscles:

1. Approach a person that you have not had much contact with (perhaps a schoolmate you don't know well, a local merchant, a person sitting next to you on the subway or bus) and give that person an opinion or belief of yours. Don't wait for a conversation to develop, just start out with . . . "I think the Yankees are going to win the pennant this year." "My favorite movie was *Star Wars*." "I don't like the way Mrs. Greene teaches math."
2. Participate in a sporting activity that you have never done before. Maybe one of these will do: logging, jump rope, ice skating, tennis, uneven parallel bars, jacks, lacrosse, dice baseball, knee basketball, jacks.
3. Write a letter with your "other" hand. Copy at least one paragraph from a book and don't quit in the middle — complete the whole thing.
4. Enter a contest or tournament in which you are not very skilled. Even if you lose or get rejected you've done something.
    — Take one of your photographs down to the local photo show.
    — Make up a recipe and enter a cooking contest.
    — Look for a contest that involves writing or drawing and give it a go. Cereal boxes, matchbook covers, backs of comic books and magazines often advertise such contests.
5. Select some physical exercise and set a goal of how much you'd like to do. Commit yourself to doing the exercise every day for, say, a month. Increase the amount you do each day until you reach your goal. *CHECK WITH A DOCTOR FIRST TO GET ADVICE AND AN OK.* Something like toe-touching, push-ups, sit-ups, chin-ups, or running in place would be good.
6. Pick an activity that you think you would be too ashamed to do and do it. *CHECK FIRST WITH YOUR PARENTS AND OTHER AUTHORITIES TO GET THEIR OK.* We know some people who tried this by:
    — calling out the stops on the subway
    — dressing up for Halloween in the middle of the summer
    — asking to borrow some money

— jumping rope in a business district during lunchtime

— walking a banana with a leash down the street

For all of them, thinking about doing it was much worse than doing it.

Some said they felt silly, but it wasn't as bad as they expected.

And some of the people were surprised by how much fun they had.

If you select an activity that you're really ashamed of doing, you'll probably *feel* the shame while you're doing it. That won't be very comfortable, but it's not the end of the world. If you start getting very upset about it, stop and find out what you're saying to yourself — maybe something like, "People are laughing at me. It's terrible. I can't take it." Then identify and challenge the irrational beliefs. Ask yourself: "Why can't I take it? I'm not going to get blown away by some laughter. It's uncomfortable, but it's not the end of my life."

Use the following chart to organize your shame-attacking activity:

What I'm Going to Do	Others' Reactions	My Feelings	My Thoughts	Challenges

Thinking Straight and Talking Sense

If you're really trying
You won't be crying that you're trying
Even if others are booing
It'll be all right
'Cause you'll be *doing.*

Complete the following A-B-C-D-E chart on procrastinating or avoiding work. (Units 10, 12, and 17 show how to develop charts like this.)

A	My Social Studies report is due in class tomorrow. It's 4:00 P.M. Sunday afternoon. All my papers and books are on my desk and the house is empty.
B	1. 2. 3.
C	I feel nervous and fidgety. I'm not able to sit down and concentrate.
D	1. 2. 3.
CE	1. 2. 3.
BE	

Questions corresponds to A, B, C, D.
Answers corresponds to CE, BE.

22 Feeling Happy — Feeling Sad

NOTES FOR TEACHERS

This unit concentrates on the idea that people can take charge of their emotions by checking on and refuting the irrational statements they are making to themselves. Although this appears to be a very simple concept, it takes constant practice to learn to overcome upsetting emotions. The reason, of course, is that most people have been taught irrational ideas practically from the day of their birth, and it takes a good deal of self-training to learn thoroughly a rational way of looking at problems of living. This unit is invaluable for people of any age — educating emotions is a useful skill for oldsters as well as youngsters and everyone in between.

Notes for Students

Many of us often say, "_____ makes us happy." Well, guess what? It doesn't. We make *ourselves* happy or sad, although it is true that things around us often *influence* us in one direction or another.

Sometimes we know *why* we feel a certain way. Sometimes we don't. This activity helps to show us how we feel and what the events and thoughts are that lead to those feelings. It asks the questions: Does something or someone other than yourself *make* you feel a certain way? Do you *have* to feel a certain way just because of the events around you?

GET in touch with your feelings by keeping a chart for the next week on the events and thoughts that occur when you feel sad and when you feel happy. Set up your chart in your notebook this way:

Feeling Happy			Feeling Sad		
Date	Event	Thought	Date	Event	Thought

Each time in the next week that you feel either happy or sad write on your chart the event, the feeling, and the thought that occurred. Remember, HAPPINESS can be many different emotions such as JOY and EXCITEMENT; and SADNESS can be MISERY, UNHAPPINESS, DEPRESSION, UPSETNESS, and BOREDOM. At the end of the week compare charts with the other people in your group.

Let's look at some items from charts of a group of sixth-, seventh-, and eighth-graders who participated in this activity:

From Feeling Happy . . .

Event: My brother didn't sleep home last night.
THOUGHT: I get the bed to myself.

Event: I was watching a funny TV program.
THOUGHT: This is better than doing dishes.

Event: I was playing jacks with my friend during a free period in school.
THOUGHT: I like Alex and I like free time.

Event: My cat had five kittens.
THOUGHT: I get to show them off.

Event: I was very happy when Joe was suspended from school.
THOUGHT: Now I'm happy that I won't get beat up any more.

Event: I found out I was going to the mountains with Abby and not Katie and Joe.
THOUGHT: It's less of a hassle with Abby.

Event: My baby cousin learned how to say my name.
THOUGHT: I'm glad when someone recognizes me.

Event: My father acted weird (dancing in front of all those people at the amusement park).
THOUGHT: Daddy's just a kid, too. If he can act silly, so can I.

Feeling Happy — Feeling Sad

Event: Charlene and I have been writing since last summer and I got a letter from her.
THOUGHT: This friendship with Charlene is working.

Now go back to each set of circumstances involving someone else and ask yourself these questions:

1. Would I feel happy with these circumstances?
2. Is it possible *not* to feel happy with these experiences? How?
3. What might I tell myself to feel happy?

   EXAMPLE: When my baby cousin learned how to say my name.
   To feel happy I might tell myself, "That's real nice that my baby cousin said my name. I guess it means she knows me and likes me."

4. What might I tell myself to feel sad?

   EXAMPLE: When my baby cousin learned how to say my name.
   To feel sad I might tell myself, "Now all I'll hear is Reggie, Reggie, Reggie. I'll have no peace. I wish she'd never learned my name."

Examples from charts of Feeling Sad include a wide range of conditions. Some might seem surprising to you for Feeling Sad. Yet, for each individual student they meant an unhappy set of circumstances. Would they be for you?

From Feeling Sad . . .
Events: I got off the plane.
I was marching in the parade.
My mother didn't understand what I was saying to her.
I called up all my old friends.
I looked at the calendar and saw that tomorrow was Monday.
I couldn't do the homework assignment.
I watched a TV program about the American Indians.
My father came home and told us we weren't moving to the new apartment.

Go back to each set of circumstances and ask yourself these questions:

1. Would I feel sad with this circumstance?
2. Is it possible not to feel sad with these experiences? How?

3. What might I tell myself to feel sad?

> EXAMPLE: I got off the plane.
> To feel sad I might tell myself, "My trip and my vacation are over and I had such a great summer. I really don't want to go back to school."

4. What might I tell myself to feel happy?

> EXAMPLE: I got off the plane.
> To feel happy I might tell myself, "Thank goodness that trip is over! What a bumpy ride! I was nauseous the whole trip. I thought it would never end."

Well, do happiness and sadness occur for *all* people in the same circumstances?

Is there any set of conditions that you could describe where everyone would feel the *same* way? Let's use an extreme example to show that it would be very unlikely.

The Conditions

You're running along a narrow path on the side of a cliff. You trip and lose your balance. You fall twenty feet to the rocks below. You're conscious but notice that one leg seems broken and the other is bleeding excessively.

What would be the "obvious" emotional reaction?

Panic? Fear? Misery? Any generally negative feeling, right?

NOT NECESSARILY.

What if you're running from people with guns and knives who are out to kill you and the fall allows you to escape your pursuers?

What if you have been a hemophiliac and your blood wouldn't clot so that any bleeding would have resulted in death, but just lately you have received treatments that help your blood to clot? You realize that, for the first time in your life, your bleeding leg need not prove fatal to you.

What if the director yells, "Cut, it's a take," and someone wipes off your make-up and you realize your role as a stunt person in this movie is complete?

Those were rather far-fetched "what ifs," so let's try a more realistic one:

You realize that your injuries are not likely to kill you, but that you need help. Worrying isn't going to help you. The important thing to do is to think calmly and decide on the measures you can take to get medical attention and prevent further damage to your body.

REMEMBER: *It's often what you tell yourself in any situation that determines how you will feel.*

For each of the following "horrible" situations create two "what ifs" — a far-fetched, fantastic one and a realistic, rational one. Make each set of conditions such that it would be easy to feel *great* about what happened.

I. You receive your score on the annual schoolwide achievement test. After speaking to your friends, you realize you have the lowest score in your class. A couple of people start calling you "dummy" and your teacher says, "Stay after school is over. I want to speak to you."

Far-fetched, fantastic "what if" _____
_____
_____
_____
_____

Realistic, rational "what if" _____
_____
_____
_____
_____

II. You open the door to your house and find the place a shambles. The furniture is knocked over. The color TV is broken. The food from the refrigerator and the cupboard is strewn all over the floor. The bathtub is running over. There is more than an inch of water on the floor all through the house. The walls have been written on with a Magic Marker.

Far-fetched, fantastic "what if" _____
_____
_____
_____
_____

Realistic, rational "what if" _____
_____
_____
_____
_____

23 Communicating Clearly

NOTES FOR TEACHERS

Much of the structure of what we call civilization has evolved through human beings' unique ability to communicate in ways that other animals cannot. Even so, it is astonishing how poorly many people communicate. In this unit we work on sorting out the difference between intentions and perceptions, and present some ways of communicating a point of view without hostility. These techniques require a lot of work. Probably the slogan "Nobody's perfect" applies almost perfectly to the area of communication.

Notes for Students

Often we plan to communicate an idea, a thought, an expectation. You know what you want to say but, when you have "communicated," you find that the people you talked to haven't heard anything you thought they would hear. The first activity in this unit can help you see the difference between intentions and perceptions (what you want to say and what they hear), and asks the questions: How can you communicate more clearly? How can you respond more openly?

INTENTION: I was just trying to be friendly.

PERCEPTION: Yeah, well you can take THAT kind of friendliness and —

INTENTIONS are what people mean to do. Here are some examples:

"I'll ask Mike if he wants me to help him because I see he's got so much to do."

"I'm going to kid Mark about being a farmer because he knows that stereotypes don't mean anything anyway and we'll have a good laugh."

"I think I'll invite Jenny to my party. She seems lonely and I know she'll like my friends."

PERCEPTIONS are the way people see things and how they feel about them because of their evaluation.

"What do you mean, help me? Don't you think I can do things for myself? You're not the only one who knows how to do things."

"Hey, I don't like your comments about farmers at all. It sounds like you're covering up your prejudice with a joke."

"No, thanks. Forget the party. I'd rather be left alone. What makes you think I need company anyway? Feeling sorry for me?"

• •

HAS it ever happened to you that you meant something one way and someone took it another way? Or people said they meant to be nice but it didn't sound so nice to you. Think about it, and then write in your notebook as many such experiences as you can remember.

Here's a list from one class:

"My teacher told me to sit near him at a music show we went to and I thought it was because he didn't trust me. So when he said it was just because he enjoyed being near me at shows like that because I enjoy them so much, I got mad."

"When we had our concert for the parents, I was supposed to stand near Wayne, but I couldn't hear the piano so I asked to move closer to the piano and he got all hurt. A couple of days before that someone had said he couldn't sing very well and he thought that's why I wanted to move."

"I smacked my uncle on his bald head because that's what a lot of kids do to people that don't have much hair. It's just a little custom — maybe to get a little attention — but he got all mad and insulted."

"Shelley was talking to Robert and I asked her to go to the store with me. Do you know, she accused me of being jealous of her and Robert and trying to get them away from each other. Well, I'm not even interested in

Robert. I'm just afraid to go to the store alone."

"When I was one of the youngest kids at a summer camp, they asked me to be in charge of making a clean-up chart for the cabin. Everyone had a job there, but it seemed to me they were just thinking young kids can only be janitors, and that's why they wanted me to do it. But when they explained it, they said it was because I was the neatest person there. And that was true. Everyone else was a slob. I got over being mad and helped shape them up."

"Every day when I would come home from school I'd find my favorite album put in the back of the stack and I know my mother doesn't really like my music so I thought she was trying to tell me something and I got madder and madder and then finally when I told her she could at least tell me instead of being sneaky she said she put it there because my little brother always played with it and she didn't want him to mess it up."

"I heard Tony and Adrian were going to have a party and I never got invited so I stopped talking to them and got real snotty. Then I found out the reason I wasn't invited was because it was supposed to be a surprise party for everyone leaving the eighth grade and I was one of them. We got it straightened out but I was embarrassed for my irrational behavior."

NOW let's try a little experiment in NOT communicating.

Write down something you are going to do for someone in your group — an act that you INTEND to be friendly, helpful, kind, supportive, funny, caring. It can be anything — a comment, an invitation, an offer.

Here's an example:

YOUR INTENTION: I'm going to ask Barbara if she wants to share my lunch because I noticed she has a small one today.

Read your INTENTION to the group and ask a couple of people what it is you intend to do. (This is the check to see if the intention is clear to everyone.)

Pair up with another person and have your partner role-play the situation with you.

The second person should take this role and play it so that his or her perception is completely opposite to your intention. For example, the second person might say

Communicating Clearly

"Share your lunch? Are you saying my mother doesn't feed me right?"

"Don't you like it? Just trying to get rid of it?"

"Poor Maria! She has to give away the only food she's got just to get some company."

Notes for Students

Well, there you have it — the big difference between INTENTIONS and PERCEPTIONS.

It can become the cause of a lot of CONFLICT: I think she thinks that I think she thinks I think she thinks.

So what can you do about it? Well, there are alternatives —

Accept the conflict and don't do anything about it

or

begin to look at it this way. Suppose you are a teacher whose job depends on whether the administrators think his or her classroom activity is effective. You could say —

I've got to make a good impression on the administrators when they visit today.

Then, when the administrators arrive, you might come up with some hysterical responses:

THOUGHT: If they see Jenny acting up the way she's doing now, they'll blame me!
Speech: Jenny, you'd better stop that now or you'll be in SERIOUS trouble with me!
THOUGHT: Oh, no! What'll I do if I can't control her?
Speech: Oh, hello, Dr. Mudge. So glad to have you here!
THOUGHT: What? he didn't like my class? Well, I really don't care. Who's he to judge?
Speech: Jenny, I'm going to KILL you!
THOUGHT: I can't STAND school! I HATE it! I'd rather be unemployed!
Speech: KIDS! SHUT UP!

Nobody won that encounter, did they? Not the kids, not the administrators, and certainly not you. Let's try it again:

THOUGHT: The administrators are coming again and I'd like to make a good impression.

This time, if the administrators appear perturbed by someone's behavior, discuss the matter with them. Tell them the history of the problem and what steps you are taking to help the people who are creating the disturbance.

STRONG responses can be ASSERTIVE . . .

"Here's my point of view. I believe in what I say, I have a stake in the outcome, and I'd like to know what you think."

(No win, no lose, I want my piece of the action and won't deny you yours.)

or AGGRESSIVE . . .

"Here's my point of view. I believe in what I say and what I do. Things are going to turn out MY way and I couldn't care less what you think!"

(We both can't win, someone's GOT to lose, and it's not going to be ME!)

Another type of response to a situation is really a "nonresponse" or what is called a PASSIVE response. Passive responses are weak. They don't often help you achieve your goals. And, because you hide your real feelings, they are dishonest. Here is an example of a passive response:

Suppose you are in a restaurant and you want to get the waiter's attention so you can change your order. You say, "Excuse me," in a very low voice. The waiter passes by and ignores you. So you say, "Excuse me, sir," in a voice that is still hardly audible. If you don't change your style to an assertive one, you are likely to get a dish you don't want.

Passive responses often occur because people believe they don't have the *right* to state assertively what they want.

We'll take a strong stand for ASSERTIVENESS as an approach that often (though not always) allows you to

express your thoughts, beliefs and feelings strongly
but
does not encourage the other person to turn off
and
reaches a compromise in which you both get a piece of the pie.

• •

WE have suggested some conflict situations below to help you practice assertiveness as a way of interacting with others.

Look at each suggested conflict situation. With another person act out a sequence of aggressive responses. Remember that we're not encouraging aggressive behavior. Rather, this should remind you that aggressive behavior doesn't usually work.

Then act out a sequence of passive responses. Again, remember that we are not encouraging passive behavior. It seldom gets you what you want either.

After you have acted out the aggressive and passive responses, discuss what each of you was thinking and feeling.

Next, brainstorm several alternative ASSERTIVE responses which will

allow you *both* to express your point of view

not attack either of you

not arouse irrational feelings such as anger, fear, or anxiety

promote a compromise solution

EXAMPLE:

Situation A

Someone steps into a cafeteria line ahead of you.

Aggressive: What the hell do you think you're doing?

Passive (While you do or say nothing, think to yourself): I wish someone would tell that guy to go to the end of the line.

Assertive (In the same clear tone you would use in giving any helpful information): Sir, the line forms back there.

Situation B

You are asking for a raise in pay. Your boss responds that the Company is laying off other people and is not giving any raises.

Aggressive _____

Passive _____

Assertive _____

Situation C

You are refusing to clean the kitchen unless someone helps you.

Aggressive _____

Passive _____
_____

Assertive _____
_____

Situation D
You are insisting that a teacher help you with your spelling even though that teacher is busy.

Aggressive _____
_____

Passive _____
_____

Assertive _____
_____

Situation E
You are trying to convince a friend to go to your favorite restaurant although she doesn't especially like it.

Aggressive _____
_____

Passive _____
_____

Assertive _____
_____

Situation F
You are trying to get someone to donate some money to your club.

Aggressive _____
_____

Passive _____
_____

Assertive _____
_____

Situation G
You are telling a friend that Pro Keds sneakers are better than Converse sneakers.

Aggressive _____
_____

Passive _____
_____

Assertive _____
_____

Situation H

You are trying to convince a librarian that you should not pay a fine on your book because you didn't get a notice.

Aggressive _____
_____

Passive _____
_____

Assertive _____
_____

Situation I

You are asking for a discount on a pair of slightly damaged shoes.

Aggressive _____
_____

Passive _____
_____

Assertive _____
_____

Situation J

You are telling someone (who disagrees) that your home town is the greatest.

Aggressive _____
_____

Passive _____
_____

Assertive _____
_____

Situation K

You are declaring that the way you take to go downtown is the best.

Aggressive _____

_____

Passive _____

_____

Assertive _____

_____

If you choose to respond assertively rather than aggressively or passively —
1. How do you feel?
2. What are you thinking?

What are the advantages of assertive responses?

After trying several assertive responses, how do you feel about "winning"? How do you feel about sharing? If you win in an interaction, what does that mean? If you share the results of an interaction, what does that mean?

24 Taking Risks

NOTES FOR TEACHERS

This unit deals with the concepts of setting goals, taking risks, and dealing with other people's disapproval, and it is a continuation of material that has been introduced in previous units. It offers many opportunities for group discussions concerning authority figures (mothers, fathers, teachers, bosses) and ways of responding to them. It also carries forward the idea of assertiveness rather than aggressiveness and, like the preceding units, promotes skills universally in demand that require continuing attention and practice to develop.

Notes for Students

Often people don't do something they want to do because they're afraid someone will disapprove. If they checked it out, they might find they were wrong about the disapproval. Or they might think the matter through and decide they were willing to go ahead and do what they wanted *even if* someone they cared about disapproved.

This activity helps us to set goals, take risks, and check out other people's reactions. It asks: Don't we often help ourselves by *risking*, even though we might *fail*? Even if someone whose opinion we value might *disapprove* of our behavior?

When you stop to think of it —

- We aren't born with most of the things we do — we learn them.
- Most people approve of what is common and expected.
- Many people don't approve of what *isn't* common and expected.
- Most people learn to do what is common and expected.

That's why you hear a lot of expressions like: YOU SHOULDN'T DO THAT! IT WON'T WORK! THAT'S NOT THE WAY IT'S DONE! WHAT WILL PEOPLE SAY? WHAT IF IT DOESN'T WORK OUT?

BUT . . .

THINGS often don't change unless someone is willing to *risk* and do something UNcommon and UNexpected.

AND . . .

Some things *are* better if changed.

SO . . .

Start with yourself.

• •

THINK of some things you'd like to change and try to guess how others will disapprove.

Start with things that are really possible — nothing too far out.

Then add the feeling you think you probably would have if they did disapprove.

Here are some examples:

What I'd Like to Do	How I Think Someone Will Disapprove	How I'd Feel If They Disapproved
I'd like to eat less, but . . .	My parents will say I'm starving myself.	I'd feel *angry* at them for not letting me do what I want.
I'd like to walk to school, but . . .	My friends will say it's too far.	I'd feel *frustrated* at not being able to show them how much fun we'd have walking.
I'd like to give up my drum lessons, but . . .	My folks will say I don't appreciate all they're doing for me.	I'd feel *trapped*.
I'd like to become friendly with a kid of another race, but . . .	Some of my friends will say I'm a traitor.	I'd feel *scared* of their rejecting me and *guilty* for not being stronger.

Taking Risks

Consider how you could deal with other people's disapproval. You might say: *So what* if others don't like what I'm doing? What do they have to say about it? If I want to do it, why not just go ahead and do it?

Be careful! That attitude might create more problems than the one you started with. You don't want to hurt or seriously inconvenience someone else. You don't want to slam the door on your relationships without thinking.

There is another way. It's the difference between acting ASSERTIVELY and AGGRESSIVELY.

What do you think, what do you feel, what do you *do* when someone says:

Oh no you don't!
I'll never speak to you again!
How could you?
You've got to be jiving!

That's really up to you, isn't it? BUT — if you want to keep the doors open, it's probably best to take your stand without beating someone else over the head.

Try saying one of these sentences or something similar:

It's something I really want to do. Give me a week.

I know you don't approve, but I can live with that if you can.

Let's see if you feel the same way a few days from now.

True, these statements aren't as dramatic as:

!*?%!

But if you're serious about your goal of (1) doing something different for yourself, and (2) keeping your relationships steady, we think you'll find this a better approach.

Now that you've written a few things you'd like to change, start with one that someone else won't see as a big hassle and give your answers to the following questions:

What is it that I want to do that I'm not doing now?
_____

Why do I want to do it? _____
_____

How important is it to me? _____

How do I think I will feel if I do it? _____

How do I think others will disapprove? _____

What will I think if they do? _____

How will I feel if they show their disapproval? _____

Will their disapproval stop me from doing it? _____

Now, go to that other person or persons and tell them directly what you plan to do and ask them what they think. Write their answer here or in your notebook.

_____
_____
_____
_____

Do they disapprove of your plan? _____

If so, do they disapprove more than, less than, or as strongly as you had imagined they would? _____

What do you think of their response? _____

How do you feel about it? _____

What did you say to them? _____

Will you still do what you planned? _____

If your answer is NO, go back and check your list of things you'd like to change. Pick another item, and run it by this list of questions. Repeat this process until you find something you will follow through. Keep a record of other people's reactions and your reactions to their reactions. Prepare a chart like this and bring it back to your group in a week:

What I'm doing that I haven't been doing _____
_____

When I did it _____
What I thought about doing it _____
_____

How I felt _____
What someone else said about it (if they said nothing, ask what they thought) _____
How I *thought* about what they said _____
_____

    Well, did it work? That is —
Did you do it? _____
Did you feel good about having done it? _____
In what way? _____
_____

Did others disapprove? _____
If so, what did they say? _____
_____

How did you respond? _____
_____

HOW DID YOU *FEEL* ABOUT THEIR DISAPPROVAL? __
_____

Will you continue doing what you began (the activity you expected others to disapprove)? _____
Why or why not? _____
_____

If you ended up feeling badly about someone's disapproval and felt that it might stop you, what could you do? _____
_____

144   *Thinking Straight and Talking Sense*

25 Errors, Goofs, and Blunders

NOTES FOR TEACHERS

This unit works on the concept that people may behave badly — but people are not bad. It also deals with the idea that people may behave well — but they are not good. It teaches the importance of judging *behavior* rather than *labeling* the individual. This approach is most important in dealing with the *self*. These ideas are the very heart of Rational-Emotive Education. We have discussed them in earlier units; the activities outlined in this unit are effective aids to understanding this important theory.

Notes for Students

Sometimes we do things we think are mistakes — or other people think they are. Then we start labeling ourselves — or others label us — as bad.

The following activity asks the question: Do lots of errors, goofs, mistakes, blunders, shortcomings, faults, and mess-ups make someone a BAD PERSON?

PRETEND you live in a world in which people rate MOST HIGHLY the people who make the MOST MISTAKES.

Some days I make so many mistakes that I'd have to be the BEST possible person in that world.

Let's see if your focusing on all these so-called NEGATIVES — recording them daily for a while — can help you believe, a little more strongly, that you are NOT any one thing that you do.

Begin a diary in your notebook of errors, goofs, mistakes, blunders, shortcomings, faults, mess-ups. Don't do something on purpose just to have it to record, but try (as most average people will be able to do) to fill page after page.

Here's an example:

I bumped into the wall.
I interrupted the teacher in class.
I cursed at my mother.
I tripped Tom by mistake.
I tore my pants.
I turned off the light while someone was still in the room.
I didn't do my chores.
I forgot to tell Barbara something important.
I got off at the wrong bus stop.
I stepped on Elaine's shoes.
I dialed the wrong number and got someone out of bed.
I've got more mistakes than you!

Yeah? Well, just wait! I feel a really crummy day coming on.

Okay, go to it. Begin your list of errors and goofs. After one week, share your findings with your class.

Here's the transcript of a discussion one class had after one week of recording:

TEACHER:	Well, how many pages of errors and goofs have you all recorded?
EDUARDO:	Seventeen.
FRANCENE:	Seventeen? I've only got four.
TANYA:	You write smaller.
GREG:	I've got eight pages, written small.
HUGH:	Eleven.
KAREN:	I tried to remember to do it, but my biggest goof of all is that I kept forgetting to do it. If I had written them all down, I'd have a lot.
TEACHER:	Well, whatever, I'd like to hear each of you read a few of yours, and I'll read some of mine, too.

(They read, with lots of groans and laughter.)

TEACHER: Okay. Now that we've focused on the so-called negatives, I'd like you to write one and only one thing you've done in the same time span that you believe you did well — a success, a victory, a high point.

(They write.)

TEACHER: What? Do you mean to say that all those mistakes didn't stop you from doing one thing well?
GREG: Not me.
TEACHER: Some people would say you're a *bad* person if you do *bad* things. But how can you be a bad person if you do one hundred so-called bad things and then are still able to do one thing well?
KAREN: You can't be all bad.
TEACHER: How could I change "I'm bad" to have it make more sense?
EDUARDO: *Sometimes I do good things and sometimes I do bad things.*

(Teacher writes it on the board.)

TEACHER: I'd say that makes a lot more sense, but who says the things you do are good or bad?
EDUARDO: Sometimes I do, sometimes somebody else does.
TEACHER: Put that into your sentence.
EDUARDO: Okay. Sometimes I do things I think are good and sometimes I do things I think are bad. Sometimes somebody else says they're good or bad.
TANYA: Everybody's got their own opinion.

WHAT DO YOU THINK?

Errors, Goofs, and Blunders

26 Dealing with Shame

NOTES FOR TEACHERS

This unit uses a very specific example to make its point. No doubt every member of your group has a personal "case history" that will be equally appropriate. In drawing out these examples from your group, you will find abundant opportunities to apply the challenging and disputing skills.

Notes for Students

Many times we find ourselves in a situation in which we really don't want to be. In order to get out of it, we may do things we regret or feel ashamed about. This activity helps us look at an example of this problem and at a way of dealing with it by using the skills we have learned in other activities. It asks the question: Even if things go badly, do you have to stay miserable?

A young man we know has been having some problems at school and at home. Four months ago he moved to a new area and started attending a very large school. Before that he had gone to a school with just thirty students — about ten in each class. He knew all of his classmates and the three teachers there very well. Now he finds himself in a large, overcrowded building with thirty-five kids in each class and dozens of teachers, none of whom seems to know his name. He had a lot of friends in his old neighborhood and would usually spend afternoons and weekends hanging out with his buddies. Each day seemed more exciting than the one before. Now at 3:30 when he gets home from school, he turns on the TV and watches it for hours on end. There are very few kids his age that live in his new neighborhood.

Has he let these things bother him?
You bet he has!
He's feeling miserable.

He has felt so unhappy in school that he is starting to cut classes. He has also begun lying to his mother. Every day when she gets home from work and asks him how's school, he says, "Fine."

"Do you have any homework?" she asks.

"No," he answers and looks away from her.

He feels a real conflict. He doesn't want to be in school and yet he's ashamed of his behavior (cutting classes and, especially, lying to his mother).

What can he do? Here are some things that have occurred to him.

- Keep doing just what he's doing. Sooner or later things will get better.
- Run away from home. There really doesn't seem to be a way out of this situation.
- Do something dangerous or illegal. Maybe someone will notice him and help him out of this mess.

We don't believe any of those ways will prove helpful. They can't help our friend feel better because they don't have anything to do with what's causing his misery in the first place. Even though he had very little to do with some of the conditions he finds himself in (moving to a new neighborhood and being in a large, crowded school), he can control his feelings. The feelings he's having now are caused mostly by his thoughts and beliefs about the situation he's in. He is making himself miserable. And one thing he can do to change this is to challenge or dispute the beliefs he has.

USING the ABC model introduced in Unit 10 and further developed in Units 12 and 17, chart how our friend's feelings of misery and shame developed.

If the beliefs aren't stated, guess what they might be.

A (Event) _____

B (Beliefs) _____

Dealing with Shame

C (Feelings) *Misery* _____

A (Event) _____

B (Beliefs) _____

C (Feelings) *Shame* _____

Now, if you decide, as our friend did, that his beliefs are irrational, you can use the challenging and disputing skills to change them. For each of the irrational beliefs listed above, ask and respond to the five challenging questions:

1. What is the irrational belief?
2. To what extent do you want to give up this belief?
3. What evidence is there to show that the belief is false?
4. Does any evidence exist of the truth of this belief?
5. Can I rationally support this belief?

It may help to review the example in Unit 10.

D (Disputing)	Questions / Answers	D (Disputing)	Questions / Answers
CE (Cognitive Effect)		CE (Cognitive Effect)	
BE (Behavioral Effect)		BE (Behavioral Effect)	

150 *Thinking Straight and Talking Sense*

Practicing these skills in problem situations can help you deal more effectively with these problems. By challenging and getting rid of your irrational beliefs you can free up energy that can be used to *do* some things about the conditions and situations you're in.

Once our friend has given up his misery and shame, he's in a much better position to deal with his school and family situation. List in your notebook a number of suggestions you would provide him to help him *do* things to change his situation. Be specific in reference to his new neighborhood, dislike of school, relationship with his mother, etc.

You might begin your list with, "If I were you, I would . . ."

27 Challenging Stereotypes

NOTES FOR TEACHERS

Conflicts caused by prejudices are prime targets for Rational-Emotive Education. In this unit we present a rational methodology for dealing with prejudice. You can use it in your group whenever there are racial or ethnic slurs or whenever people judge by category instead of by considering individual behavior.

Notes for Students

A stereotype is an image or description applied to *all* members of a certain group. It is true that people in groups share *some* characteristics. However, a stereotype greatly exaggerates what's common and ignores what's unique and individual. Thinking in stereotypes often results in dangerous conclusions. Much harm has been done to members of certain groups because of stereotyping thinking.

This unit presents a way of challenging stereotypes. It asks the question: If I belong to a group (such as cultural, racial, religious, social, physical), does it mean that I must possess all the characteristics of the other members of the group?

A stereotype (or any irrational belief) can be challenged and disproved by asking questions:

1. Do all members of this group have this characteristic? (If the answer is NO, the stereotype is disproved.)
2. Is there any member of this group that does not have this characteristic? (This is a variation — different form — of question 1.)

3. Are there others outside this group who also have this characteristic? (If the answer is YES, the stereotype is weakened and made easier to disprove.)

4. What are the definitions of the terms in the stereotype and are they agreed upon by most people? (Answering this question changes the statement into behavioral or more correct language and the stereotype is weakened and destroyed.)

Let's see how these four questions to challenge stereotypes work.

THE STATEMENT: *Jewish people have big noses.*
THE QUESTIONS:

1. Do all Jewish people have big noses.

Yes ____ No ____

2. Are there *any* Jewish people who do not have big noses? Yes ____ No ____

3. Are there members of other ethnic groups who have big noses? Yes ____ No ____

4. Who is Jewish? _____

Many different types of people consider themselves Jewish — Kirk Douglas, Moshe Dayan, Sammy Davis, Jr., Dinah Shore, and Vidal Sassoon "are" Jewish.

What are the definitions of the terms? How "big" is a big nose? It depends on how you define big.

THE CONCLUSION: The statement "Jewish people have big noses" is a stereotype — unprovable and untruthful as it stands.

ALTERNATIVE STATEMENTS:
Some Jewish people have big noses.
Larry has a big nose.
Patty's nose is bigger than mine.
The average length of fourteen Jewish people's noses that I measured was 2.31 inches long.
I think Jewish people have longer noses than Irish people, but I can't prove it.

Challenging Stereotypes

APPLY to the following statement the method we used above to challenge stereotypes.

THE STATEMENT: *Tall boys are good basketball players.*

THE QUESTIONS:

1. Are all tall boys good basketball players?

   Yes ____ No ____

2. Are there any tall boys who are not good basketball players? Yes ____ No ____

3. Are there other people (for example, short boys or tall girls) who are good basketball players?

   Yes ____ No ____

4. What qualities make a good basketball player? Are there other things than being tall that make someone a good basketball player? Yes ____ No ____

THE CONCLUSION: _____
_____
_____

ALTERNATIVE STATEMENTS:
_____
_____
_____
_____
_____
_____

As long as you can find one member of the group who does not fit the statement about the group, then you have proved that the statement is a stereotype and, therefore, not true.

Mark McBane, a black kid, used to believe that all white kids are prejudiced until he met Sean Peterson, a white kid. Mark saw that Sean didn't act in a prejudiced way, became good friends with him, and proved that the belief, "All white kids are prejudiced," is a stereotype and, therefore, not true.

Alicia Takada told us that up until the fifth grade she thought that girls are smarter than boys because, in every class she had been in, the girls got higher marks. In her fifth-grade class, Ronald Murphy and Butch Kirk got the best report cards. Now Alicia realizes that the statement, "Girls are smarter than boys," is a stereotype and, therefore, not true.

Try this: Choose a very general statement about a group. Look for words like *always, all, every*, and forms of the verb *to be* (like *is* and *are*). It's easy to find statements like that. Just listen to people talk! "Kids are ... " "Teenagers are ... " "Girls are ... " "Boys are ... " "People are ... " Or watch television — especially the commercials — and you'll hear a lot of very general statements. Then find one member of the group for whom the statement is not true.

Get into the habit of challenging your stereotypes and those of other people. We believe it is a practice that will help in your relations with others and in your thinking and well being.

28 Winning and Losing

NOTES FOR TEACHERS

Here is another look at the problems created by insisting on being "Number One." There is a good opportunity here to review the earlier units on setting goals and sticking to them. You can place that idea in the perspective of winning and losing, succeeding and failing. Again the emphasis is on trying and learning to take risks, with self-acceptance regardless of the outcome of the effort.

Notes for Students

We're all part of a society that often tells us: BEST IS BEST! Tops is best! First is best! Biggest is best! Strongest is best! Smartest is best!

For many of us, it's fine when we *win*, but very hard when we *lose*. This unit helps us look at other ways of thinking and asks the questions: Why must I be best at everything I do? Does being best at something make me good?

Consider all of these phrases that refer to forms of competition: First in line! Most popular! Chosen for the team! Best dressed! Top of the class! All A's! High potential! Most points! Best-looking! Going places!

One obvious point here is that everyone can't be first, and people can make themselves quite unhappy by thinking that they have to be the one at the top. In the narrative below, an adult tells how he made himself miserable in his teens by his outlook on winning and losing.

LOOKING BACK AT MY TEENS

When I was a teen-ager, I kept a secret checklist of my "wins" and "losses." The day was a good one or a bad one depending on how many points I got.

	Points
Bob H. talked to me.	10
Miss Edwards asked me to go to the office for her (and didn't ask Mary Lou B.).	10
Terri S. said she liked my shirt more than Jim K's.	10
I didn't get picked for the basketball game in the gym.	minus 50
I got an A on the social studies quiz (almost everyone got lower).	25

It was me *against* the others. I went to bed plotting for the next day:
What can I do to make Miss Edwards pay attention to me?
How can I get a compliment on my appearance?
What can I do to get out of gym so I won't be rejected again?
Is there a way I can get a good grade in math and still stay on the good side of the "bad" guys?

My plan became my trap. There was never enough time or energy to stop the enemy — losing. So I'd get praised by the teacher and put down by the guys. Then I'd do something to bring up my status with the guys and Mary Lou would call me a fool. Trying to convince Mary Lou that I was no fool took a lot of time and when the next homework assignment didn't get done it was back to losing points with Miss Edwards. The hassles with her put me on the run again with the guys and Mary Lou. Back to the planning board — three hours' sleep . . . upset stomach . . . nails bitten to the elbow.

"Now let's see — if I tell her. . . . No, that won't work. Maybe if — but then she'll say. . . . Oh, I know. . . . No. . . . What if . . . ?"

What was behind all of this?

"I've got to win!"

"If I don't, I'm no good at all!"

"If I do, I'm terrific!"

"I couldn't take it if I didn't get what I want!"

"People have got to like me!"

"People had better like me!"

"I don't think I can handle this all but, if I can't, somebody will find out I can't and they won't like me, so I'd better pretend I can handle it all, even if I can't, and then they'll never know. But what if they find out . . . what happened?"

Winning and Losing

Well, I did win sometimes and I lost sometimes, too. I had lots of struggles with myself and with others, but I made it through. Here I am, alive and still growing. All the TERRIBLE, HORRIBLE, AWFUL things that were supposed to happen because I was weak, unsure, unwanted, uncool — they never really happened. What could I have done to help myself along the way?

I could have looked at my beliefs, perhaps using the questions listed in the activity below.

I could have looked at the *real* possible consequences of winning and losing by answering the following questions:

What's the BEST that could happen if _____
_____?

What will PROBABLY happen if _____
_____?

What's the WORST that could happen if _____
_____?

I could have asked, "EVEN IF the worst happened, *would* it be horrible?" And if I answered, "Yes," I could have asked, "What's the evidence?"

• • • • • • • • • • • • • • • • • • • •

ON a 1 to 10 scale (10 for the greatest belief, 1 for the smallest belief) show how much you believe in the following statements:

1. Some people are better than others. ____
2. First is best. ____
3. Biggest is best. ____
4. Strongest is best. ____
5. Smartest is best. ____
6. It's better to win than to lose. ____
7. You're rotten if you're not first, biggest, strongest, smartest. ____
8. It's a terrible thing if I lose. ____
9. I can be best if I try hard enough. ____
10. People who are the best during their life get a big trophy when they die. ____

Notes for Students

Here are some of the things we have come to believe about situations like this:

There is no absolute *best*.

First, biggest, strongest, and *smartest* change with the context.

Just because you're *first, biggest, strongest, smartest* in one situation doesn't mean you will be in all situations.

We all win some. We all lose some.

You are not *good* or *bad* depending on whether you win or lose.

What is most important is doing and believing what helps us to feel good about ourselves.

We can often help ourselves by *not* worrying about winning or losing but by using our energy *to perform as well as possible in areas that we consider important.*

Support from and for others is usually more helpful than competing with each other.

Even if we can't change the attitudes about winning and losing that surround us, we can change our own.

Feeling disappointed or hurt about losing is very different from feeling shattered, torn up, or rotten.

PREPARE an A-B-C-D-E chart on a situation in which you ended up far from the top. It may be helpful to review Units 10, 12, and 17.

Winning and Losing

29 Making a Game of Insults

NOTES FOR TEACHERS

This unit continues the work begun earlier on dealing with other people's negative comments and responses. Point out the difference between totally ignoring a negative comment and examining it to see if it offers a useful suggestion for improvement (even if it is put in a very destructive form). Once your group accepts the fact that everyone makes mistakes and that many people help themselves by recognizing their errors and learning from them instead of simply writing themselves off as worthless, they can begin to deal with negative comments as matters to be weighed for possible merit rather than as total indictments. Here again we suggest a *course of action* as opposed to paralyzing self-pity or anger.

Notes for Students

We all have many characteristics that are not perfect. If we already feel badly about one of them, we often feel worse if someone makes a negative comment about it. The activity in this unit helps us to see how we can defend ourselves from other people's negative comments about us by not thinking so negatively about ourselves. It asks: Who upsets us — other people or ourselves?

First, let's talk about insults.

An insult is an insult only if the person who is the subject of comment takes it as an insult.

Suppose someone says: YOU'RE UGLY! Now, if you don't take the intended insult as an insult, it's not an insult. Here are some answers Janet Thomas thought of in response to YOU'RE UGLY!

"So?"

"I'm ugly, eh? I'll bet there's something else he doesn't like about me. I wonder what it is."

"Well, that puts me in some pretty good company. People said Eleanor Roosevelt, Abe Lincoln, and Boris Karloff were ugly, but they seemed to do okay."

"I'll just ignore that comment."

"Well, you're entitled to your opinion."

"Isn't that interesting? Several people have told me the same thing, but I don't think so at all."

"Big deal! Ugly schmugly! Who cares?"

"Well, maybe I am, but what does that mean?"

"Is what you call ugly something you don't like about the bones in my face? Is it something I was born with and can't do a whole lot about? Or are you talking about something I can change for the better?"

"Yeah. You know, I agree. But this is the only face I've got and I've learned to love it. Do you love yourself as much?"

"Ugly is beautiful!"

Janet didn't take "You're ugly" as an insult — she protected herself from feeling badly. It might seem a little unrealistic now, but sooner or later she might ask:

What does it mean to be ugly?

Are there any so-called ugly people who have not let ugliness stand in their way?

Do I believe in ugly?

Do I think I'm ugly?

THIS game can help you deal a little better with so-called insults. Here are the rules:

Rule Number 1 is to agree to follow the rules.

State a characteristic about yourself that you will allow others to try to insult.

Everyone in the group takes a turn at trying to insult you. (You're only the first target. Everyone else will take a turn at parrying "insults" soon enough.)

In this dialogue, no one may curse or mention any other family member. No counter-insults are allowed.

When you are "insulted," try to:

(a) ignore or

(b) respond positively or neutrally

Give yourself *one* point for ignoring, responding

Making a Game of Insults

positively or neutrally, and *minus one* for responding negatively. Keep a record.

Here is an example:

Darlene - Your nose looks like a banana.
Mack - Thanks. I love bananas. *(One point)*

Alfred - You're a rhinoceros, aren't you?
Mack - No, but I know a very friendly one. *(One point)*

Rachel - You don't ever run out of breath with *that* nose, do you?
Mack - No, it's a good one. *(One point)*

Jenny - That's a nose? I thought it was a cucumber!
Mack - *(Ignore) (One point)*

Ruth - That's the most horrible looking nose I ever saw in my life!
Mack - You don't have to enjoy being hateful and mean so much! *(Subtract one point)*

Duane, Wayne, and Corey tossed insults at Mack, too, and he responded. His record chart looked like this:

Name: Mack
Characteristic: Big nose

	Responses			
	Negative	*Ignore*	*Neutral*	*Positive*
Darlene				x
Alfred				x
Rachel				x
Jenny		x		
Ruth	x			
Duane			x	
Wayne				x
Corey		x		

Number of insults: 8   Score: 7 − 1 = 6

Notes for Students

Are we saying: INSULTS ARE GOOD!
NO!

We are saying that we can control what we think of other people's *intended* insults and we do ourselves a favor if we ignore them, or think positively or neutrally about them. Sometimes it helps to practice a new response, even if at first it seems a little phony. Sooner or later the only thing that will *really* help is if we *believe* what we think and what we say. Maybe acting as if we believe can help us learn to believe.

One class we know did this activity and said:

"It was fun. I think insults are pretty dumb, but I used to get upset."

"If I think they're right (when they try to insult me), I might take it a little serious but not like before. Now I don't get so upset."

"We used to do it a lot and get upset and it was kind of fun but someone was always getting hurt. So now it's kind of boring because you don't believe them any more."

"It's a good exercise because now I don't think I've got to keep proving stuff to people."

How do you feel about other people's negative comments now that you have done this activity? Do insults *have* to make you feel bad?

30 Facing Complications

NOTES FOR TEACHERS

> The activity that follows deals with those times in people's lives when they feel that everything is falling apart. Fortunately, for most people this doesn't happen often. But when it does, it usually seems pretty bad. REE suggests ways of helping deal more rationally with ourselves and the problem at hand. It presents an opportunity to practice helping someone whose life seems very complicated and it asks — and answers — the question, "Why *must* our lives be without complications?"

Notes for Students

What can you do when things go wrong? Has it ever seemed to you that when one thing goes wrong everything goes wrong? Just wait till you hear the story of Emerald Kee. Maybe it will remind you of complications in your life.

Emerald Kee had had a pretty good life. Her first eleven years had been usually happy and relatively simple. THEN SHE TURNED TWELVE! It seemed from the day of her twelfth birthday (September 6th) that her life started going crazy. Her birthday fell on the first day of school. She was starting the seventh grade at Bryant Junior High School. Elementary school had been a snap for Emerald. She always got A's, had a lot of friends, and the teachers all knew her and seemed to like her. Then KABOOM! She walked into Bryant and asked the first kid she saw, "Where's Room 223?" The kid, a girl about two heads taller than Emerald, pushed her against the wall and said, "Don't talk to me, girlie, or I'll get you after school." When Emerald finally did get to Room 223, she was told to go back to the attendance office on the first floor and get a late pass. Before that eventful day was over, Emerald

- lost her house keys.
- got more homework assignments than she had gotten in the entire sixth grade.
- was yelled at by two teachers, a hall monitor, and the lunchroom lady.
- was pushed around and threatened after school by the same girl she met in the morning.
- forgot to pick up her sister Grace from kindergarten.
- lost her babysitting job for Saturday night.
- fell off her bicycle and hurt her left leg.

It was just the beginning.

Now, three months later, Emerald can hardly remember when things were not complicated. It seems nothing in her life is easy any more. She finds school very difficult. Most of the teachers don't even explain what they assign for class and homework. The girl who threatened her the first day of school bothers her at least two or three times a week. There are racial problems at Bryant, and most of the kids seem more uptight than they were in elementary school. Among her friends, things are also very complex. No longer does she see and hang around with the same two girls she always did, Tara and Ruth. Tara goes to Catholic school now and is never around. Ruth has started hanging out with a fast crowd, smokes, cuts classes, and is always with tough older boys. And speaking of boys, Emerald is shocked at how disgusting some of them act since they've started at Bryant. They're always talking about each other's mother, insulting people, talking loud, cursing, and telling dirty jokes. On the other hand, there's Carl Zen. Emerald really likes him but every time she's with him she notices that Carl seems embarrassed, and usually walks away from her with some kind of lame excuse. The rest of her life is equally unsettling. She smoked her first cigarette last week and, although she didn't like the taste too much, she's been thinking about smoking a lot since then. Although she knows her parents love each other, she's become very aware of the arguments they have — mostly about money. She's thought about getting a job as a C.I.T. in a day camp for the summer, but doesn't really know how to start and thinks she might be too young.

All of these aspects of her life and the beliefs and feelings about them have been a little confusing to Emerald. Sometimes she feels really badly and wonders why things can't be easier. Why must her life be so complicated? she asks.

— Imagine that you're a friend of Emerald's. She wants to talk over all that has been happening outside and inside of her.
— Use the ABC model of emotions and the five challenging questions, as well as a sharing of support and concern, to respond to the following statements:

Don't worry about being right (there's no one right way). Just take a chance.

Emerald: I absolutely can't stand to hear my parents argue about money. It makes me so unhappy.
You:
Emerald: I'm so angry I'm gonna kill that girl at school if she bothers me one more time.
You:
Emerald: I don't understand why Carl always runs away from me. I'm sure he doesn't like me. I feel like an idiot for chasing after him.
You:
Emerald: I am so frustrated with my English teacher. She never answers a question. I hate her.
You:
Emerald: Sometimes I think I'm going crazy. I wish I was really young again and I didn't have to deal with all these complications. Things were so easy then.
You:

In helping Emerald work through her problems, use the challenging questions that were presented in Unit 12. They are:

1. What is the irrational belief? Define it. State it in the way you're saying it to yourself.
2. How much do you want to give up this belief? How willing are you to work at the challenging and disputing?
3. What proof is there to show that the belief is false (irrational)?
4. Does any evidence exist of the truth of this belief?
5. Can I rationally support this belief?

Use the introductory sections on the ABC's in Units 10 and 12 to help Emerald challenge and dispute her irrational beliefs.

31 Using Your Imagination

NOTES FOR TEACHERS

We hope you will enjoy this unit as much as your class will. The activities and suggestions included here can help you to arrive at creative solutions for yourself as well as your class.

Notes for Students

MYTHS • FOLK TALES • LEGENDS
MYSTERIES • TALL TALES • FABLES
PARABLES • ALLEGORIES

Literature is full of events, adventures, and exploits that never really happened or that sort of happened but are exaggerated way beyond the truth. So what? They are fun, exciting, fascinating and — as long as we know they're not totally for real — how can they harm us? As a matter of fact, they just might help us in some ways.

Let's take a look at how a legend grows. We start with a set of basic *facts*:

Diane was walking home from school one day and she saw a woman trying to get into her locked house. She had the wrong keys and couldn't open the door, so she asked Diane to crawl through a small window. Diane did, opened the door from the inside, let the woman in, and went on her way. Coincidentally, two days later the same things happened with the same woman.

Now, consider "The Legend of Diane Salerno."

Once upon a time, Diane Salerno, a small, unknown school girl, was walking along the street minding her own business, thinking of ways she could have fun once she got home. Diane may have looked ordinary on the outside, but her dreams made her one unusual little girl. She dreamed of greatness, grandeur, being a heroine. Today seemed like an average day, but little did Diane know that this was the day her new world would begin. As she passed 1234 Roosevelt Street, she saw a woman fumbling with her keys, trying to open the door to her house. She seemed greatly distressed.

"May I help?" asked Diane.

"I wish you could," replied the woman, "but I have the wrong keys."

"Are there any windows open?" Diane inquired.

"Not a one," the woman answered. "They're all locked and bolted."

Suddenly Diane felt a great surge of strength in her body. "Let me try the door," she suggested.

"Little girl, I already told you that I have the wrong key."

"I know," replied Diane, "but I didn't say, 'Let me try the key.' I said, 'Let me try the door!'"

With that she grasped the handle and the door opened.

The woman gasped. "Who are you, little girl? And where do you get your strength?"

From that day on Diane was known as "The Girl Who Can Open Any Door." Her legend will never die.

• • • • • • • • • • • • • • • • • • • •

ACTIVITY

WELL, how about you? Could you make up a legend, myth, fable, or tale about yourself? Following these steps will help you:

Write about, tell about, or tape a real happening in your life in which you performed in a strong, noticeable, or unusual way. Here are examples of topics that some people have selected.

- the time I sank six baskets in a row
- the time I stayed up all night without falling asleep
- the time I ate eleven pieces of pizza
- the time I sat for four straight hours listening to music
- the time I walked thirty-seven blocks from home to a discount store just to buy some socks

- the time I took care of my baby brother all day after my mother went to the hospital
- the time I walked for the first time with my body brace
- the time I caught a ten-pound carp
- the time I grew three inches in two months
- the time I walked all the way to the top of the Washington Monument
- the time my drawing was chosen and I was asked to do part of the mural for the library

Now, start thinking of this one event and begin to *exaggerate* it. You might say it didn't just happen once, but a lot of times ... it made a big difference in other people's lives ... you became famous for it. Whatever you think, think of extremes.

Next, get together in a group so that everybody can help you build your legend. One teacher we know uses suggestions like these to help stir students' imaginations:

So you were on your eleventh piece of pizza ...
What suddenly appeared?
What did the pizza turn into?
What did the pizza say?
What did you suddenly become?

Or the teacher suggests that the students make up a new fact about the story that has to do with a color, a temperature, a smell, a sound, a motion, a song, a building, or some other element that will add interest.

Sometimes if the students are really stuck, the teacher will help even more by making up new, outrageous facts to get them started. Here are some of them:

So, as I was getting ready to bite into the eleventh piece of pizza, a small voice suddenly called out from under a mushroom and said ...
or
I bit into the pizza and the next thing I knew I was lying back down on a sea of tomato sauce, tied to a raft made of sausage with heavy strands of mozzarella cheese. Then ...

Well, whatever you do, work out a story full of exaggeration, surprise, absurdity, humor.

Once you have a pretty good story going orally, retell it and tape it or write it down. One class we know

Using Your Imagination

has done these things to complete and share their stories:

- wrote them on ditto and made copies for everyone in the class to read
- made up comprehension questions on their own stories for the rest of the class
- made wall posters of their stories
- turned their stories into a scripted dramatization and had several people act it out for the class
- created an illustrated story by taking a series of photographs of the action and mounting and captioning them
- taped the stories read by several people and added the cassettes to the class listening center

Notes for Students

So, what does this have to do with Rational-Emotive Education?

One important thing, we think: You always have lots of CHOICES . . . OPTIONS . . . ALTERNATIVES.

Usually there are many more than you see. Often when you're in the middle of a PROBLEM . . . DILEMMA . . . HASSLE, all you can see is what is there and you cannot see any way out. Learning to use our FANTASIES . . . IMAGINATIONS . . . CREATIVITY . . . can help us see things we never saw before and open up SOLUTIONS we wouldn't have seen otherwise. Sometimes the RIDICULOUS can lead to the POSSIBLE.

Here's an example of what we mean: One group spent a couple of weeks on the fantasy activity we described above, making up terrific legends and myths and talks about themselves. Then a real problem came up and the teacher proposed the same method to help solve it. This is a report of what happened:

The teacher said to the class: All right, here's our problem. Everybody in the class wants to take trips but we don't have any money and there is no one to supervise the group except me. Let's just pretend there are *no limits* on how we solve it.

The first question is: Who can help us?

The class suggested the President, Muhammed Ali, Fonzie, the Mayor, Jerry's grandmother, Frankenstein, Millie Jackson, Ella Grasso, Mrs. Jakubowski, John Travolta, and lots more.

A class member wrote down all the possibilities on the board.

Then the teacher asked for suggestions on how to get in touch with them. Again the suggestions from the class were noted on the blackboard: letter, paper airplane, shout, radio ad, TV ad, billboard, code, whisper, newspaper article, satellite, photos, and so on.

The next question was: What will we ask them? Some of the answers were:

Can we come visit you?
Will you give us some money?
Will you come visit us?
Where did you go on trips when you were a kid?
Do you want to bring a group of yours to our school?
Do you have a bus we can borrow?
Do you want to come with us somewhere?

Now the teacher asked: What can we suggest we do? And the class responded:

Let's have dinner together.
Let's play basketball.
Let us interview you.
Let's interview someone else together.
Let's go swimming.
Let's go to the library.
Let's bake something.
Let's build something.
Let's paint something.

They worked on these lists of possibilities over several days using these rules:

1. Any suggestion counts. Don't criticize any.
2. Try to come up with as many suggestions as possible.
3. Build onto someone else's idea.

We won't give you every detail of what happened, but here's the outcome.

After a few days they went through each list and decided what they could *realistically* do. They surprised themselves when they realized they had many more choices than they had thought they had. Taking a couple more days, they finally came up with this plan — believe it or not!

They wrote a letter to about twenty-five people in their community and to a few of their favorite famous people.

Dear _____:

We are a sixth-grade class at _____ School. We

would like to go on trips to learn more about the real world, but we can't afford it and we don't have anyone to go with except our teacher. We would like you to help us, but first we would like to help you. Would you come to our class for dinner on Monday, December 8, at 6:00? We will serve chili and cornbread and Jello and coffee. We are making everything ourselves. Then we would like to talk to you about helping us take trips. Let us know if you are coming . . .

Well, thirteen people came, including a well-known legislator. Those guests formed a committee and in the next two months, with parents' permission, a number of them accompanied the class to a radio station, museum, restaurant, and gymnastics tournament, providing car transportation three times and arranging public transportation once.

Everyone involved thought it was a pretty good match of people. And it all began by using the good old imagination to exaggerate the truth.

That's one of the things that REE is all about — discovering more CHOICES . . . OPTIONS . . . ALTERNATIVES than you ever dreamed of. And acting on them.

Try it yourself.

32 Looking Ahead

NOTES FOR TEACHERS

This is the final unit in this book. It carries forward the ideas we have worked on earlier about self-understanding and defining goals. A week or several weeks could be devoted profitably to this unit.

Notes for Students

By now we hope you have a clearer idea of what you do . . . what you think . . . how you feel . . . some things you can do to change yourself.

This course has offered you some tools which will help you work out A PLAN FOR THE FUTURE.

START out with some general questions and answer each in three ways:

1. A reasonable, practical answer — something you could *really* do.
2. An *ideal* answer — something you could do, and would like to do, but might have a lot of trouble with.
3. A *fantasy* answer — something way beyond your ideal.

Here's an example from Rodney:

Question: What physical condition might you expect to be in three years from now?
Answers from Rodney:

1. I'll be about the same as right now but a little stronger.
2. I'll be a lot stronger than now so I won't get tired swimming or playing ball and I won't get sick either.

3. I'll be the strongest kid in the world and every germ would stay away because they'd know they couldn't get in.

Here are our general questions. Use your notebook to answer each one in the three ways we have suggested and add some of your own.

1. What physical condition will you be in?
2. What kind of food will you eat?
3. What kind of exercise will you participate in?
4. How will you look?
5. What will your daily schedule be?
6. How much will you sleep?
7. Where will you live?
8. Whom will you live with?
9. How many and what kind of friends will you have?
10. How well known will you be?
11. What plans for the future will you be making?
12. What formal learning will you be participating in?
13. What will your most unusual trait or activity be?
14. What will others think of you?
15. What will you think of others?
16. What will be your greatest problem?

Notes for Students

This activity really got our group to thinking, especially when we shared our answers. It helped us think more clearly about WHAT'S IMPORTANT TO US . . . WHAT'S NOT SO IMPORTANT TO US . . . WHAT WE WANT TO CHANGE . . . WHAT WE *CAN* CHANGE.

We decided to apply these insights and what we had learned from our other activities in making a specific plan for a goal. We worked it out in great detail and, at last count, many of us *were* following through — *not perfectly*, of course, but enough so that it feels as if we're moving and growing — not just standing still.

A PLAN FOR THE FUTURE

The characteristic, thought, fact, or condition I am going to consider changing is _____

Now go through the following questions and circle the answers you think are most nearly correct:

Is it something I *can* change? YES   NO

If your answer is NO, start again until you can answer YES.

How hard do I think it will be to change?
VERY   SOMEWHAT   NOT VERY   NOT AT ALL

Is it something I *want* to change? YES   NO

If your answer is NO, go back to the beginning, pick a new subject for change, and keep working through these questions until you can find a subject for change to which you can answer YES.

How much do I want to change it?
A LOT   SOMEWHAT   NOT MUCH   NOT AT ALL

If you answer NOT MUCH or NOT AT ALL, it would probably be a good idea to start again until you can answer A LOT or SOMEWHAT.

Got it? All right, now go ahead with this plan:

Plan Period

From _____ to _____
      (date)   (date)

Present Situation

Now I _____

_____

I think _____

_____ about the situation.

I feel _____

_____ about the situation.

Goal

By _____ I want _____
   (date)

_____

Forces

Ones I Can Control	Ones I Can't Control
_____	_____
_____	_____
_____	_____
_____	_____

Thoughts

Ones I Can Control	Ones That Will Hold Me Back
_____	_____
_____	_____
_____	_____
_____	_____

Steps (Mini-Goals)

1. _____
2. _____
3. _____
4. _____
5. _____
6. _____
7. _____

(Seven is no magic number for your mini-goals. You may need more or fewer. Check each when done. Add any necessary ones.)

Thoughts About Plan

_____
_____
_____

Feelings About Plan

_____
_____
_____

Evaluation - End of Goal Period

Did I reach my goal? _____
Did my plan help me? _____
In what ways did it or didn't it? _____
_____
_____

How This Course Evolved

Rational-Emotive Education, true to the basic tenet of its parent, Rational-Emotive Therapy — that most *absolutes* get us into a lot of trouble — suggests *some* cognitive-affective techniques and approaches for helping *some* students and teachers *some* of the time. Our evidence is that the *somes* are increasing.

We have presented in this book a program in Rational-Emotive Education, a philosophic and methodological approach toward the integration of affective and cognitive concerns into a school curriculum. Our work for the past few years has provided most of the material on which the book is based. In the summer of 1974 we were hired by the Institute for Advanced Study in Rational Psychotherapy (now the Institute for Rational-Emotive Therapy) to serve as the staff of The Living School. The Living School, creation of Dr. Albert Ellis, had been in existence since 1969. Its purpose was to develop and establish an emotional education program that would be used mainly in elementary and junior high schools, based on the theory and practice of Rational-Emotive Therapy. The main principle of RET — that it is our beliefs about things that create our feelings and not the things themselves — had been widely acknowledged and practiced as a leading cognitive therapeutic approach with adults. With the establishment of The Living School the focus broadened to include work with young people, emphasizing preventive critical-thinking skills. For a number of years, under the leadership of Dr. William Knaus, The Living School adapted the adult individual and group therapy model to work with children. Dr. Knaus's *Rational-Emotive Education Manual* (1974) describes the use of such an approach.

How did the plan change along the way? _____
_____

How did the plan affect other people? _____
_____

Which steps helped most? _____
_____
_____

Which steps helped least? _____
_____
_____

How do I feel about the plan now? _____
_____

How do I feel about the goal? _____
_____

Do I think the goal was completely reached? _____
If not, do I plan to continue working toward it? _____
If so, what is my new plan? _____
_____

If I reached my goal, what does that mean? _____
_____

If I didn't reach my goal, what does that mean? _____
_____

Danny, one of our students, said after looking back over a plan in which he only partially reached his goal, "Well, it's better to have risked and lost than never to have risked at all."

What do you think?

In our first year at The Living School we realized that a need for the preventive emotional education skills still existed. Our twenty-one students helped us through the early development of the lessons, activities, contests, and charts that comprise the curriculum of this book. We have devoted the past several years to refining and elaborating this curriculum through consultations at elementary and junior high schools, workshops for educators and parents on the theory and practice of Rational-Emotive Education, and interaction with relatives, friends, and colleagues on the content and style of the material we've written.

This book is the result of those efforts.

Reading List

AVAILABLE FROM IRL

The following materials may be obtained from the Institute for Rational Living, 45 East 65th Street, New York, New York 10021.

BOOKS

Bedford, S., *Instant Replay.* New York: Institute for Rational Living, 1974.
Berger, Terry. *I Have Feelings.* New York: Human Sciences Press, 1971.
Ellis, Albert. *How to Live With — and Without — Anger.* New York: Reader's Digest Press, 1977.
Ellis, Albert. *How to Live With a Neurotic.* New York: Crown, 1975.
Ellis, Albert. *Humanistic Psychotherapy: The Rational-Emotive Approach.* New York: McGraw-Hill, 1973.
Ellis, Albert. *Reason and Emotion in Psychotherapy.* Secaucus, N.J.: Citadel Press, 1977.
Ellis, Albert, and Grieger, Russell. *Handbook of Rational-Emotive Therapy.* New York: Springer, 1977.
Ellis, Albert, and Robert A. Harper. *A New Guide to Rational Living.* North Hollywood, California: Wilshire Books, 1975.
Ellis, Albert, Janet Wolfe, and Sandra Moseley. *How to Raise an Emotionally Healthy, Happy Child.* North Hollywood, California: Wilshire Books, 1966.

Garcia, Edward, and Nina Pellegrini. *Homer, the Homely Hound Dog.* New York: Institute for Rational Living, 1974.
Hauck, Paul. *The Rational Management of Children.* New York: Libra, 1967.
Knaus, William. *Rational-Emotive Education: A Manual for Elementary School Teachers.* New York: Institute for Rational Living, 1974.
Maultsby, Maxie, Jr. *Help Yourself to Happiness.* New York: Institute for Rational Living, 1975.
Merrifield, Calvin. *Call Me RET-Man and Have a Ball.* (Comic Book) New York: Institute for Rational Living, 1979.
Waters, Virginia. *Color Us Rational* (12 stories to read, 50 pictures to color). New York: Institute for Rational Living, 1979.
Waters, Virginia. *Rational Parenting Booklet Series* (6 booklets for parents and 6 stories for children). New York: Institute for Rational Living, 1980.
Young, Howard. *Rational Counseling Primer.* New York: Institute for Rational Living, 1974.

TAPE RECORDINGS (Cassettes)

Ellis, Albert. *Conquering the Dire Need for Love.*
Ellis, Albert. *Conquering Low Frustration Tolerance.*
Ellis, Albert. *I'd Like to Stop, But . . . Dealing With Addictions.*
Lazarus, Arnold. *Learning to Relax.*
Ellis, Albert. *RET and Assertiveness Training.*
Ellis, Albert. *Rational Living in an Irrational World.*
Ellis, Albert. *Theory and Practice of Rational-Emotive Psychotherapy.*
Ellis, Albert. *Twenty-One Ways to Stop Worrying.*

VIDEOTAPE

Eyman, William, and Gerald, Mark (with introductions to lessons by Virginia Waters). *Teaching Rational-Emotive Education to Children.* (10 lessons drawn from classroom sessions of The Living School)

AVAILABLE FROM GENERAL SOURCES

The following books may be obtained from general sources such as libraries, bookstores, and publishers.

Ashton-Warner, Sylvia. *Teacher.* New York: Simon and Schuster, Inc., 1963.
Barnes, Ellen, Eyman, Bill, and Bragar, Maddy. *Teach and Reach.* Syracuse, New York: Human Policy Press, 1977.
Braun, Carl, and Froese, Victor (eds.). *An Experience-Based Approach to Language and Reading.* Baltimore: University Park Press, 1977.
Brown, Cynthia. *Literacy in Thirty Hours.* London, England: Writers and Readers Publishing Cooperative.
Brown, Rosellen, et al. (eds.). *The Whole Word Catalogue.* New York: Teachers and Writers Collaborative, 1972.

Burns, Marilyn. *The Book of Think: Or How to Solve Problems Twice Your Size.* Boston: Little, Brown and Co., 1976.

De Bono, Edward. *The Five-Day Course in Thinking.* Harmondsworth, Middlesex, England: Penguin Books Ltd., 1976.

Dillon, J. T. *Personal Teaching.* Columbus, Ohio: Charles E. Merrill Publishing Company, 1971.

Dollar, Bruce, and Parker, Thomas. "Students as producers of their own learning," *Social Policy,* 8(3), November-December, 1977, pp. 69-72.

Fader, Daniel. *The Naked Children.* New York: Bantam Books, Inc., 1972.

Fluck, Sandra. *Experiential English.* London, England: Collier-Macmillan, 1973.

Gartner, Alan, Riessman, Frank, and Kohler, Mary C. *Children Teach Children.* New York: Harper and Row, 1971.

Glasser, William. *Schools Without Failure.* New York: Harper and Row, 1969.

Gordon, Sol, and Conant, Roger. *You! The Teenage Survival Book.* New York: Times Books, 1975.

Gordon, William J. J. *The Metaphorical Way of Knowing and Learning.* Cambridge: Porpoise Books, 1971.

Gordon, William J. J. *Synectics.* New York: Harper and Row, 1961.

Gordon, William J. J., and Poze, Tony. "Learning, dysfunction and connection." *Psychiatric Annals,* 8(3), March 1978, pp. 79-88.

Hawley, Robert C., et al. *Composition for Personal Growth.* New York: Hart Publishing Co., Inc., 1973.

Holt, John. *Instead of Education.* New York: Dell Publishing Co., Inc., 1976.

Illich, Ivan. *Deschooling Society.* New York: Harper and Row, 1970.

Jones, W. Ron. *De-School Primer No. 4.* San Francisco: Zephyrus Exchange.

Jones, W. Ron. *Finding Community: A Guide to Community Research and Action.* San Francisco: Zephyrus Exchange.

Kohl, Herbert. *On Teaching.* New York: Bantam Books, 1976.

Krantz, Shelley. "The impact of experiential learning," *Media and Methods,* September, 1977.

Mosier, Doris, and Park, Ruth. *Teacher-Therapist: A Handbook for Teachers of Emotionally Impaired Students.* Salt Lake City, Goodyear, 1979.

Padgett, Ron, and Zavatsky, Bill. *The Whole Word Catalogue 2.* New York: Teachers and Writers Collaborative, 1976.

Perone, Vito. "Documenting teaching and learning," *Social Policy,* September-October, 1977.

Piaget, Jean. *To Understand Is to Invent.* Harmondsworth, Middlesex, England: Penguin Books Ltd., 1976.

Wigginton, Eliot. "The Foxfire approach: It can work for you," *Media and Methods,* 14(3), November, 1977, pp. 48 ff.

Acknowledgments

Many people have contributed to the work on this book and supported us in myriad ways during its development. We would like to thank them all.

Albert Ellis, Janet Wolfe, and the **Board of Trustees** of the Institute for Rational Living — for providing us, through our employment in the emotional education division of the Institute, with the opportunity for writing this book.

Dorothy Arfer, Administrative Director of the Institute — for her concern, support, and numerous instances of kindness that we deeply appreciated and still do.

Ginger Waters, staff psychotherapist at the Institute — for her thoughtful consultations, consistency, and persistence, and for her clarification of the concepts of Rational-Emotive Therapy.

Madelaine Riley, Bill Dunn, Dan Beck, Susan Arfer, and **Jean Simon,** our co-workers at the Institute — for all the help, praise and criticism, patience, and humor that highlighted our work days.

Laini — for her love, encouragement, and partnership in this project as in many others.

Jessica and Benjamin — for providing a great sense of confidence for future emotional health.

All the kids from the Living School (**Jenny, Aubery, Manny, Reggie, Michele, Richard, Michael, Abby, Judd, Cherie, Sean, Mark, Elissa, Beth, Tony, Nigel, Ursula, Charlie, Menzena, Willie, Wana**) — for starting out with us on this venture from the beginning, teaching us a lot about Rational-Emotive Therapy, and vividly demonstrating the challenges and rewards of teaching.

Richard Wessler, Barbara Sansone, Richard Harris, and **Easy Zimmerman** — for inspiring a number of activities presented in this book, and helping us to clarify the relationship between education and therapy.

Stanley Elson — for his enthusiasm, cooperation, "goodness," jump shot, and scallops with abalone mushrooms.

Merili Geller — a teacher of unique enthusiasm and belief in people's ability to learn and grow.

Larry Levine — for his special interest and his acting on that interest so that he often questioned and challenged our work and almost always improved it.

John Blangiardo and his staff in District 22 (**Ira Roth, Tom Tropea, Judy Gold, Mitch Gruber, Patty Miller**) — for taking a chance with our material at a critical stage in its development, and our special thanks to John, for his sincerity and dependability and for "putting down the rock."

Gerry Segal, Kathy Howe, and **Ersilia Eastman** — educators who helped us in our development of the material.

The Humanness Test Force at Clinton Junior High School (**Alex, Cheryl, Richard, Lisa, Ellyn,** and **John**) — for what they taught us and what they learned about problem-solving.

The students at Hudde Junior High School (**Rose, Larry, Harry, Cecilia, Craig, Betsey, Hector, Diane, Yvonne, Aaron, Katrina, Joanne, Michael**) — a hand-selected group of students whose friendliness, cooperation, and intelligence helped make the audio video project a pleasurable experience for us.

Bland Carr — for his interest and openness, a human being who inspires reason and emotion by the way he lives.

Valerie Evans — for helping greatly with many of the activities in the book by applying them to her own life . . . a real "learner."

Ernest Watson — for the many lunches we shared and his helpful perceptions of the concepts and techniques of Rational-Emotive Education.

Marianne Wickel (so much more than just an expert audio video person, former educator, and therapist-in-training) — for being a real pleasure to work with.

Beth Wayson — who helped compile the Reading List.

The many students, teachers, and workshop participants — for the dynamic give-and-take that characterized our consultations, demonstrations, and workshops, without which this book would have presented more armchair philosophy than the intensely practical, rigorously tested concepts and methods we offer here.

● ●

About the Authors

Mark Gerald enjoyed his childhood growing up in the Bronx, New York. School, family, and the streets all contributed to his early education and he continues to find opportunities for learning in many diverse (both formal and informal) activities. He has taught elementary and junior high school students in New York City and Oxnard, California, and has worked in the drug addiction field as a teacher, counselor, and vocational rehabilitation consultant. He is particularly interested in counseling and psychotherapy, especially as those skills relate to normal developmental problems in people's lives, and is currently working toward his Ph.D. in counseling psychology. He lives in Manhattan, New York, with his wife, Laini, and their children, Jessica and Benjamin.

William Eyman says he wishes he had had this book when he was growing up in Lorain, Ohio, in the 1940's and 1950's, where the connection between thinking and feeling (to the best of his recollection) was never considered. He thanks his sixth-grade students at Croton Elementary School in Syracuse, New York, in 1967, for the breakthrough experience in which he learned the cognitive-affective link and began to develop methods to help children learn that they can shape, in varying degrees, their view of events and perhaps the events themselves. He has worked since that time in public and alternative schools, and presently in a community mental health center, applying that lesson to his life and to the lives of children. He lives in Providence, Rhode Island.